The Innocence of Dreams

Psychoanalysis Observed (ed.)
Anxiety and Neurosis
A Critical Dictionary of Psychoanalysis
Imagination and Reality
Reich
Psychoanalysis and Beyond
(*edited by Peter Fuller*)
Viewpoints

The Innocence
of Dreams

CHARLES RYCROFT

The Hogarth Press
LONDON

Published in 1991 by
The Hogarth Press
An imprint of
Chatto & Windus
20 Vauxhall Bridge Road
London SW1V 2SA

First published in 1979 by The Hogarth Press Ltd

A CIP catalogue record for this book is available from the British Library.

ISBN 0 7012 0915 1

Printed in Finland by
Werner Söderström Oy

Contents

CONTENTS

Acknowledgements

Books, unlike dreams, do not write themselves, and the ideas expressed in this one have been gleaned from many sources, some of which I remember, some of which I have forgotten, and yet others of which have become so much part of me that I have, on occasion, to remind myself that I cannot always have held them. The task of tracking these influences down would be time-consuming and tedious, and I have only recorded in the Notes the immediate sources of ideas I am using or referring to.

Nor do I intend to saddle any of my relatives, friends, colleagues, teachers or pupils with even a hint of responsibility for this book. I must, however, thank the various analysts who have listened to my dreams and the many analysands who have told me theirs. Two of the former receive credits at appropriate places in the text, while I must apologize to those of the latter, none of whose dreams I have quoted; and also to the man who was rash enough to tell me one of his dreams while propping up a bar, and also too to a young woman I have never met, whose therapist told me one of her dreams during a supervision session. Both will, I hope, forgive me.

I am fortunate in being able to make the conventional gestures of gratitude to my wife with perfect sincerity, and I thank her not only for her understanding, encouragement and forbearance but also for her skill in creating diversions.

Preface to New Edition

Although initially I had no special interest in dreams, I discovered early on in my analytical career that I seemed to have a certain facility for understanding them, by which I mean that my patients seemed to find it helpful to tell me their dreams and to take heed of my comments on them. At first I attributed this fact, if it was one, to my having thoroughly absorbed Freud's writings on dreams, but as the years went on I came to suspect that I was making assumptions about their nature and function which differed significantly from those made by Freud.

As a result, I welcomed the opportunity given me by the Hogarth Press and Pantheon Books to write a book about dreams and thereby discover what I really did think about them. As a first step in doing so, I had, of course, to return to Freud's writings and there I discovered that he made a number of assumptions about dreams which have not stood the test of time. Perhaps the most striking of these was that dreams are specific events constructed to deal with specific contingencies. According to Freudian theory a dream is the (usually disguised) hallucinatory fulfilment of a (usually unacceptable) wish which is threatening to disturb sleep and its function is to express and dispose of the disturbing wish so that sleep can continue—the implication being that 'normally' or 'ideally' sleep is dreamless. This may, perhaps, have been a plausible assumption in the 1890s when Freud was writing his *The Interpretation of Dreams*, but has ceased to be a tenable one since 1953, when Aserinsky and Kleitman discovered that there are two phases or types of sleep and that in one of them dreaming is continuous—and, further, that we all spend between a half and a fifth of our sleeping time dreaming.

PREFACE

The fact that everyone dreams every night and that, indeed, dream deprivation can be induced by persistently waking people up while they are in the dreaming phase of sleep, also makes untenable Freud's idea that dreams are, or are analogous to, neurotic symptoms. If everyone dreams every night, dreaming must be a normal function and Freud's characterization of them as 'abnormal psychical phenomena' akin to hysterical phobias, obsessions and delusions must be a category error.

In my book *The Innocence of Dreams* I have spelled out in detail the implications of assuming that dreaming is imaginative activity occurring during sleep, imagination being that function or faculty which enables us to remember what has happened, to envisage what has yet to happen, to imagine things that may or could never happen, and to use images of one set of things to make statements about something else, i.e. to use metaphor. Assuming, following Susanne Langer, that symbolization is a natural activity of mind, not a defensive manoeuvre designed to conceal meaning, I have described how dreams can be regarded as metaphorical messages from one part of the self to another, typically from a wider self to the conscious ego; how these messages are expressed in non-discursive symbolism (i.e. in [mostly] visual imagery not language), using metaphors largely derived from body symbolism (i.e. using metaphors based on the resemblances that can be discerned between human bodily parts and processes and the 'not-self' external world of natural objects, animals and artifacts); and how the art of interpreting dreams depends on the interpreter's intuitive capacity to perceive the similarity between things that are in other ways dissimilar. In asserting that dream interpretation is based on intuitive understanding of metaphor, I run counter to Freud's natural-scientific bias, which led him to assert that intuition 'is exempt from all criticism and consequently its findings have no claim to credibility.' (*Standard Edition*, IV, p 350.)

This view of dreaming, which in many ways bears a close

resemblance to the traditional, literary view, raises questions about the identity of the dreamer, since it assumes the existence of both an active agent who creates and sends dream messages and a passive recipient who receives or 'has' dreams, about the content of the messages sent by the dreaming agent, and about the reasons why so many dream messages are unremembered, unheeded and ununderstood. It implies, I argue, the existence of some mental entity which is more preoccupied with the individual's total life span and destiny than is the conscious ego with its day-to-day involvement with immediate contingencies, and which not uncommonly encounters blank incomprehension from an ego which is unprepared to admit that its conception of itself may be incomplete and misguided.

It also implies that dreams are innocent in the sense that they lack knowingness, display an indifference to received categories, and have a core which cannot but be sincere and is uncontaminated by the self-conscious will. My title, *The Innocence of Dreams*, alludes both to Blake's *Songs of Innocence and of Experience* and to G.K. Chesterton's *The Innocence of Father Brown*, whose simplicity of vision enabled him to solve mysteries.

Finally, I must make it clear that my book is neither anti-Freudian not anti-Jungian. It is Jungian to the extent that it dispenses with Freudian metapsychology and regards dreams as messages from a wider self, but Freudian to the extent that it regards the body as a main source of dream imagery and maintains that the major concern of the dreaming self is the individual's biological destiny—his inheritance, genetic and social, from his parents, his survival and fulfilment as an autonomous person, his recreation and continuation of himself as an actual or symbolic parent. But my book's main message is that dreams are best understood if one ceases to think of them as discrete phenomena or events but instead responds to them as momentary glimpses of the dreamer's total imaginative fabric, into which are woven all his memories, expectations, wishes and fears.

The Language of the Dream/Night is contrary to that of Waking/the day. It is a language of Images and Sensations, the various dialects of which are far less different from each other, than the various Day-Languages of Nations.

Samuel Taylor Coleridge, *Notebooks*

Dreams, as everyone knows, may be confused, unintelligible or positively nonsensical, what they say may contradict all that we know of reality, and we behave in them like insane people, since, so long as we are dreaming, we attribute objective reality to the contents of the dream.

Sigmund Freud, *An Outline of Psycho-Analysis*

The language of poetry is not a human effort to express emotion, but emotion's expression of itself.

Kuo Mo-Jo, quoted by David Tod Roy in
Kuo Mo-Jo: The Early Years

Introduction

Presumably men and women have always had dreams, have been stirred by some of them, and have on occasion told them to others. It is, however, only within the present century that dreams have aroused serious scientific interest and have been regarded as being as deserving of investigation as the shared, objective world we perceive when awake. This delay in the emergence of a scientific interest in dreams was due, it seems, not primarily to the lack of technical devices with which to study them, but to the fact that there is something about them that makes them inherently resistant to the scientific method, at least as generally understood. The natural sciences concern themselves with phenomena which can be observed by more than one person and which either continue to exist through extensive periods of time or recur under predictable conditions. But dreams can only be observed by the single person who dreams them; the objects that appear to be visible during them have only fleeting existence; and although they may be remembered, they cannot be observed a second time. There is no going back to have a second look at a dream or asking a colleague to confirm that we have observed it correctly.

Dreams, in fact, lack that quality which would enable one to call them things, even though they accord to the *Shorter Oxford English Dictionary* definition of a phenomenon as 'That of which the senses or the mind directly takes note'. As a result, if one insists, as Freud did and most contemporary psychoanalysts still do, on calling them phenomena or events, they have to be distinguished from other phenomena and events by being designated 'subjective' or 'mental'. But even calling dreams subjective phenomena is a fiction, an intellectual ruse or device, the function of which is to enable one to talk about them as if they were the same sort of phenomena as the things we see and observe while awake, as if they were things we perceive, when they are really activities of our own. Calling dreams phenomena is, in fact, a device for overcoming their resistiveness to the scientific method by treating the activity of a subject as though it were an object he had perceived.

It is, however, possible to think about dreams in quite another way, as I hope to show in the main text of this book. This is that dreams are not phenomena we observe but experiences we have and create for ourselves, and that the appearance of objectivity presented by them is an illusion arising from two sources: first, from the fact that we have thoughts and feelings for which we wish to disown responsibility; and secondly, from the fact that we think, feel and imagine in many different modes at the same time and have difficulty in being conscious of them all at the same time—and, more specifically, that being members of a culture which sets high value on reason and verbal ability we may have difficulty in recognizing our visual, concrete imaginings as our own thoughts.

The fact that dreams are experiences which can be categorized as phenomena despite being imaginative creations of the dreamer himself, and which feel 'real' despite being undemonstrable to anyone else, was responsible for the centuries-long neglect of dreams by scientists. According to the American analyst, B. D. Lewin, the history of science started with an explicit exclusion of dreams from the field with which scientists could legitimately concern themselves. 'Around the year 500 B.C. natural science began with a repudiation of the dream. Heracleitos of Ephesos issued a scientific manifesto in the two sentences: "We must not act and speak like sleepers, for in our sleep too we act and speak" and "The waking have one world in common, but the sleeping turn aside each into a world of his own." '[1]

The second sentence quoted by Lewin from Heracleitos describes clearly and simply both the fascination and the intellectual difficulties created by dreams. While dreaming we appear to enter a world of our own. In it we appear to be doing all kinds of exciting, frightening, horrifying, delightful or absurd and impossible things. We can return to the selves we once were and to the places we once knew. Or we can become what we hope or once hoped to become—or what we fear or once feared we might become. But we can share none of this with anyone else. We can, it is true, tell our dreams to someone else and, if we are lucky, his imaginative response to them may give us the illusion of a shared experience. But if the person we tell a dream to turns out to be a sceptic, we have no means of convincing him that we really did have the dream we have told him. If he asks for proof that we had that precise dream and no other one, that we have remembered it correctly, we cannot give it. We cannot ask the people who appeared in the dream to confirm our story. Unlike the events of everyday life, which can, in principle, be confirmed or otherwise by the laws of evidence, and unlike the events of our intimate personal relationships, which can be confirmed or otherwise by reference to the identical or reciprocal responses of the other, dream experiences have a peculiar privacy about them, which can only be partially and often only self-deceptively reduced by recounting them to others.

In view of this peculiar, private quality of dreams, it is hardly surprising that the majority of scientists prior to Freud steered clear of them, regarding them as trivia undeserving of serious attention. However, as I discuss briefly in the main text of this book, in ancient and medieval times, when it was widely, if not universally, believed that mental images did not just refer to objects but were, or corresponded to, them in some real sense, dreams were taken seriously, even by the educated and scholarly. In a world in which even educated people accepted classical, and later, Christian cosmology as literally true, and those few who did not mostly kept their mouths shut, and in which, therefore, belief in the existence of angels, demons, ghosts and spirits, and in the real possiblity of visitations by

3

benign spirits and possession by the Devil, was endorsed by the general consensus, it can hardly have been superstitious or neurotic to entertain the idea that the dead could visit one in a dream or that one could receive prophetic messages during sleep. But with the rise of rationalism following the Scientific Revolution of the seventeenth century, which was accompanied, at least in Protestant countries, by a loss of belief in the literal truth of Christian cosmology even by the religious, dreams fell into an intellectual limbo; as private, subjective and fleeting occurrences, they were resistant to the natural scientific method, while the loss of nerve of the religious in respect of their belief in the objective presence of spirits meant that they no longer cited dreams as evidence of the reality of the spiritual world.

However, when Freud, after a fashion, succeeded in applying natural scientific modes of thought to dreams and by doing so made an interest in them intellectually respectable, the precise way in which he did so turned out to have a number of unexpected and misleading consequences. First, by categorizing dreams as phenomena, he succeeded in formulating scientific laws applicable to them, but at the cost of ignoring the dreamer who dreams them; and also at the cost of conflating cause and meaning. As I pointed out in an earlier essay[2], if dreams have meaning and can be interpreted, they must be creations of a person or agent who endows them with meaning, while if they are phenomena with causes they must be explicable in terms of prior events without reference to an agent. One cannot really have it both ways, and the attempt to do so leads only to confusion.

Secondly, by categorizing dreams as 'abnormal psychical phenomena' (see p. 8 below) he succeeded in explaining them to his own satisfaction as analogous to neurotic symptoms, but at the cost of obliterating the distinction between health and illness. If dreams are both universally occurring experiences and abnormal psychical phenomena, then the healthy are virtual neurotics, and the distinction between health and

4

wholeness on the one hand and illness and lack of integration on the other goes by the board. And furthermore, if, as Freud agreed, there is some connection between dreams and the waking imagination, then imagination must also be an abnormal psychic phenomenon, since if imagination resembles dreams and dreams resemble neurotic symptoms, then imagination and its products must be the expression and result of neurotic conflict, and works of art which are humanly admired for their beauty and truth become scientifically only explicable in terms implying pathology, thereby conflating admiration and disparagement, excellence and illness.

In various sections of this book I have sought to disentangle some of the confusions to which Freud's attempt to capture dreams for science by treating them as subjective phenomena analogous to the symptoms of illness has given rise. And throughout it I have adopted a position in many ways the opposite of his, assuming that imagination is a natural, normal activity of an agent or self, and that dreaming is its sleeping form, while recognizing that conflicts within the imagining self, or between different aspects or parts of the self, will manifest themselves in dreams which can only be understood if one assumes that the dreamer has been in two minds as to whether he wants to understand his dream—or whether he wants his dream to be understood—and has, therefore, used symbolism to disguise, not reveal, meaning in the way held by Freud to be characteristic of all dreams. It is my conviction that the approach I have adopted has two merits: it clarifies the theory of dreams by removing from it tortuosities that arose from Freud's attempts to explain a normal activity in language designed for illness; and by likening dreams to waking imaginative activity it makes available for dream interpretation insights about the nature and function of metaphor with which writers and literary critics have long been familiar.

I open, as is both logical and fitting, with critical expositions of the theories of dreams held by the two founding fathers of depth psychology, Freud and Jung, but readers unfamiliar with psychoanalytical terminology will do better to start with Chapters 3 and 4 and then return to Chapters 1 and 2 to discover to what extent the imaginative theory of dreams I am proposing both differs from and resembles those of Freud and Jung. The difficulty is basically with Freud's theory, or rather with the conceptual framework he used. It requires, I believe, a degree of acclimatization to accustom oneself to descriptions of subjective experiences couched in language which suggests that they are movements of energy within an apparatus, but it seems to be impossible to discuss Freud's ideas without temporarily becoming entangled in *his* metaphorical system.

In Chapter 5 I discuss various types of dreams, including those which arouse general curiosity, those with which many readers will themselves be familiar, and some which are of particular theoretical interest. In Chapter 6 I discuss the physiology of sleep and dreams, leaning heavily on the research that has been going on in dream laboratories during the last twenty-five years, and have done so with an eye on the extent to which this research does or does not confirm existing psychological theories of dreams, and is or is not compatible with my own.

In Chapter 7 I discuss the relationship of dreaming to the culture within which the dreamer lives, using as my example the effects on dreaming and attitudes towards dreams of the Scientific Revolution, which converted our own culture from one which explained everything mundane and physical by reference to the purposes of a supreme mind above to one which seeks to explain everything mental by reference to physical causes below—which reversed the direction of explanation, so that wholes had to be explained by reference to their parts, the higher by reference to the lower, instead of, as previously, the other way round. This example seems to me to be of particular interest for two reasons: first, because the earlier standpoint still survives among the religious and, indeed, in all of us who have absorbed the art and literature of the past; and secondly, because recent developments, such as cybernetics and communication theory, suggest the emergence of a new synthesis in which purpose and cause, human agency and impersonal events, mind and matter, will become reconciliable.[3]

Chapter 9, although written in a different key to the others, should be read as a recapitulation of the main theme of this book and not as a coda to it.

Finally, I must explain my use of the word 'innocence' in the title. I refer not to any presumed ignorance on the part of dreamers, nor to any presumed freedom from guilt—on the contrary I would maintain that while dreaming we may know more than we know while awake and may voice thoughts and wishes that evoke guilt when we awaken—but rather to the idea that dreams lack knowingness, display an indifference to received categories, and have a core which cannot but be sincere and is uncontaminated by the self-conscious will.

CHAPTER 1

Freud's Theory of Dreams

Introductory

Freud maintained that dreams are neurotic symptoms or, to be more precise, are analogous to neurotic symptoms inasmuch as they are constructed by the same psychological mechanisms despite the fact that they occur not only in neurotic but also in healthy persons. As he put it in the preface to the first edition of *The Interpretation of Dreams* (1900):

> For psychological investigation shows that the dream is the first member of a class of abnormal psychical phenomena of which further members, such as hysterical phobias, obsessions and delusions, are bound for practical reasons to be a matter of concern to physicians.[1]

The psychological mechanisms which are, in Freud's view, common to both dreams and neurotic symptoms are discussed critically in the following sections of this chapter. But, briefly, Freud's idea was that dreams are a compromise between, on the one hand, wishes that have been repressed and, on the other hand, the restrictions on open expression of these wishes imposed by the repressing agency; and that, furthermore, this compromise is expressed in hallucinatory form, so that the repressed wishes are represented as fulfilled but in terms or images which ensure that their nature is not revealed: '. . . the content of a dream is the representation of a fulfilled wish and . . . its obscurity is due to alterations in repressed material made by the censorship . . .'[2] He also held that most of the dreams of adults express repressed erotic wishes and that the function of dreaming is to preserve sleep—in much the same way as the function of neurotic symptoms is to preserve waking equanimity.

Furthermore, he held that dreams and neurotic symptoms reveal the existence of a mode or type of mental activity very unlike that which characterizes waking thinking. This mode, which Freud called the primary process, consists of the mechanisms of condensation and displacement—which are discussed in detail on p. 14 ff and 16 ff below—takes no cognisance of the categories of space and time, and generates not actions but wish-fulfilling hallucinations. In Freud's view these primary processes are primitive and archaic, development of the capacity for adaptive, rational thought and action only occurs insofar as they are repressed, and dreams and neurotic symptoms betoken failures of repression. In a later section I discuss Freud's concept of the primary and secondary processes and give my reasons for thinking that it should be replaced by that of discursive and non-discursive symbolism.

According to Freud, then, dreams are, in principle at least, abnormal phenomena, and are specific events and constructions, not simply mental activity continuing during sleep and occasionally glimpsed by consciousness. They fulfil a specific function, that of preserving sleep, and they express in hallucinatory but disguised form forbidden wishes that have been repressed. Much of this book is an enquiry into the extent to which Freud was or was not right in his view of dreams.

The Wish-fulfilment Theory

According to Freud (1900)[3], dreams are essentially hallucinatory fulfilments of wishes which, if they remained undreamt, would awaken the sleeper. Since, however, overtly wish-fulfilling dreams are a rarity, Freud postulated the existence of some mental agency which forbad the open expression of wishes which it found unacceptable or offensive, repressed them, and insisted on distortion of the dream imagery into unrecognizable and incomprehensible form whenever the repressed wish began to express itself during sleep. This mental agency he named first the Censor and later the Super-Ego.

In Freud's view, then, any particular dream is likely to be a compromise between a repressed wish which, if unexpressed, would awaken the sleeper and a censoring, repressing agency forbidding its open expression—the compromise being achieved by expressing the repressed wish in veiled terms, so that, as a result, the offensive repressed wish is, temporarily at least, disposed of and discharged without the dreamer becoming aware of its nature and meaning.

If dreams are disguised hallucinatory fulfilments of repressed wishes, it follows that their meaning can only be discovered by interpretation, i.e. by unscrambling the distortions imposed by the censor, and that when interpreted, dreams turn out to express wishes that are in some way offensive to the dreamer's self-esteem or moral values: death wishes towards loved ones, perverse, incestuous or infantile sexual inclinations, or wishes revealing a greater degree of egotism or pride than the dreamer likes to think of himself as possessing.

Of the two types of dreams which are most obviously resistant to explanation by the wish-fulfilment theory, traumatic dreams (see Chapter 5, p. 98) and anxious dreams (see Chapter 5, p. 103), the former were always admitted to be exceptions to the theory, while the latter were explained as failures to achieve an acceptable compromise, so that the under-lying, repressed wish came too near to open expression for comfort. Furthermore, at the time that Freud formulated his theory of dreams, he also held that anxiety was a manifestation of repressed libido[4], an idea which increased the plausibility of his theory by converting an apparently obvious objection to it into an argument in its favour. If anxiety was transformed libido, then anxiety in a dream was evidence that it contained a repressed wish. I shall return to this point later (Chapter 5, p. 107 ff).

Since manifestly wish-fulfilling dreams are a rarity, Freud's insistence on the theory is puzzling unless one realizes that his interest in dreams was not initially on their own account but as examples of a general psychological tendency towards wishful thinking and hallucinatory gratification, a tendency also exemplified by neurotic symptoms, which were, he believed, also compromises between repressed wishes and resistances against expressing them.

Although contemporary Freudian analysts still subscribe to the view that there is a general human tendency towards wishful thinking and hallucinatory gratification, I doubt whether many still consider that ascertaining the underlying wish in a dream constitutes the essence of dream interpretation. They are more likely to assume that dreams represent the total psychological state of affairs existing at the time the dream is dreamt, and that figures appearing in dreams are as likely to symbolize aspects of the dreamer's own personality as to represent 'objects' towards whom the dreamer entertains repressed wishes. Heterosexual dreams may, for instance, be interpreted as representations of attempts to integrate masculine and feminine aspects of the dreamer's personality and not as hallucinatory wish-fulfilments of the dreamer's sexual longings towards the 'object' depicted in the dream.

Although Freud's original wish-fulfilment theory of dreams has been largely abandoned by analysts, or, perhaps better, incorporated into a complex, structural view of dreams, of which the wish-fulfilling tendency of thought plays only a part, the theory still survives as a popular myth—often coupled with the implication that wishes expressed in dreams are more authentic than the counter-wishes which have prevented them being acted upon, or even recognized in waking life.

Finally, the wish-fulfilment theory of dreams assumes that dreams have an expressive, abreactive function and does not allow for the possibility of their being integrative or communicative activities.

The Primary and Secondary Processes

Freud's major theoretical contribution to the understanding of dreams was his idea that the mind works in two sharply opposed ways, one of which is exemplified in dreaming, the other in conscious thinking. There are, he maintained, two types of mental functioning, the primary and secondary processes;[5] the former being characterized by condensation, displacement, and symbolization, obliviousness to the categories of space and time, and the relief of instinctual tension by wish-fulfilling hallucinations occuring, prototypically, in sleep as dreams; the latter, the secondary processes, being governed by the laws of grammar and formal logic and respect for the categories of space and time, and leading to the relief of instinctual tension by learned adaptive behaviour. It was, furthermore, his view that the primary processes precede the secondary processes—hence the terminology—and that all ego-development and acquisition of secondary process thinking capacity is contingent on repression of the primary processes. As a result, he held that the primary processes are archaic, primitive and maladaptive, and that dreaming is in principle a neurotic symptom, since it betokens the existence of primitive wishes striving for hallucinatory fulfilment, despite the repression to which they have been subjected.

This part of Freudian theory suffers, to my mind, from four serious defects. First, conceptualization of dreaming as a symptom can only be squared with the fact that everyone dreams by arguing, as Freud indeed did, that everyone is neurotic; an ironically attractive idea, but also one which renders useless the distinction between health and neurosis (see pp. 27–29).

Secondly, the assumption that ego-development and the acquisition of the capacity for rational, secondary process thinking depends on repression of the primary processes implies that human beings enter the world totally unadapted to meet it, an inherently improbable assumption which is not in accord with the biological and ethological evidence, and one which raises insoluble problems of ontogeny. If we started life as 'a chaos, a cauldron full of seething excitations' with 'no organization'[6] and given to satisfying our wishes by hallucination, it is hard to imagine how we could begin to experience the external world in such a way as to learn adaptation from it. This difficulty does not arise if one assumes that both processes co-exist from the beginning of life, that they both have adaptive functions, and that they are not necessarily in conflict with one another—even though they may on occasion be.[7]

Thirdly, the assumption that the primary processes are intrinsically primitive, maladaptive, irrational, unrealistic and anarchic, in contrast to the intrinsically civilized, adaptive, rational and realistic secondary processes, left Freud no option but to categorize imagination, creative activity and even intuition and emotion as in principle neurotic, regressive and symptom-like—a position which, as is well known, caused Freud and the early analysts considerable trouble, and from which Freud himself eventually though reluctantly retreated. 'Before the problem of the creative artist analysis must, alas, lay down its arms' (Freud 1928).[8]

Fourthly, Freud's formulations of the theory of the primary and secondary processes are part and parcel of his mechanistic assumption that the mind is a mental apparatus within which energy circulates, the two processes being indeed essentially, in Freud's view, differing ways in which mental energy moves or remains static within different parts of the apparatus. Unfortunately, however, we really have no idea what mental energy is or what the concept means.[9] As a result, I have throughout this book only used those of Freud's concepts, e.g. condensation and displacement, which can be restated in terms of the humanist concept 'meaning', and have followed Susanne Langer in assuming that symbolization is a basic human need, not a symptom produced by conflict and repression, and that human behaviour is a language, not a set of mechanisms for discharging tensions. One effect of my doing this has been the use of Susanne Langer's terms non-discursive and discursive symbolism to make distinctions between different types of thinking which orthodox Freudian analysts make by referring to the primary and secondary processes.

The following quotation from Susanne Langer's *Philosophy in a New Key* spells out in detail the differences between discursive and non-discursive symbolism.

> Language in the strict sense is essentially discursive; it has permanent units of meaning which are combinable into larger units; it has fixed equivalences that make definition and translation possible; its connotations are general, so that it requires non-verbal acts, like pointing, looking, or emphatic voice-inflections, to assign denotations to its terms. In all these salient characters it differs from wordless symbolism, which is non-discursive and untranslatable, does not allow of definitions within its own system, and cannot convey generalities. The meanings given through language are successively understood, and gathered into a whole by the process called discourse; the meanings of all other symbolic elements that compose a larger, articulate symbol are understood only through the meaning of the whole, through their relations within the total structure. Their very functioning as symbols depends on the fact that they are involved in a simultaneous, integral presentation.[10]

A pure example of discursive symbolism would be a sentence all the words of which possessed exact dictionary definitions and would lose or change meaning if the order of the words were changed. A pure example of non-discursive symbolism would be a dream in which all the images appeared simultaneously and it was a matter of indifference to the dreamer in which order he described them.

Condensation

This is the process or device by which two or more images are fused to form a composite image which has meaning derived

14

from both (or all)—or which means that which is common to both. In Freudian theory it is one of the primary processes characteristic of unconscious thinking.

An example: a young man dreamt that he was falling headlong into some machinery which, on investigation, proved to be a composite of the threshing machine and the electricity generating plant which had been familiar sights on his father's farm. At the time of the dream he had been in danger of adopting a profession of his father's choice, and the dream image of machinery condenses the two sources of his father's hold over him: his prestige as his father and his erstwhile right to punish him.

Condensation of people occurs commonly in dreams, so that a person may be simultaneously the dreamer's father and husband, wife and mother, his present employer and his former teacher, his analyst and one or other of his parents, etc—the reference being in every case to that which is common in the dreamer's attitude towards both.

For similar reasons, condensations of sexual organs also occur, leading to images of penile breasts, vaginal and anal mouths, and even anal breasts and vaginal penises.

Some analysts, for example Ella Sharpe in her *Dream Analysis*,[11] also use the term 'condensation' to describe the fact that dreams tend to be shorter than their interpretation, i.e. that it takes fewer words to describe a dream than to explicate its interpretation, and that single details in dreams may allude to several topics or themes. In this sense, condensation describes the non-discursive quality of dreams, a quality they share with poems, jokes, music and paintings, in which the various themes, points, meanings are not spelled out serially as in indicative and expository prose but are interwoven or presented simultaneously.

This way of looking at the matter assumes, however, that prosaic, discursive formulations are the norm and that poetic, dreamy, representational, non-discursive formulations are special cases which require explanation by invoking some

15

specific process, viz condensation, to account for the transformation of prosaic thoughts into dreams. But it could in fact well be the other way round; it could be that the primary mode of mentation is representational and non-discursive and that we have to learn how to spell out or explicate before we can convert non-discursive imaginative activity into verbal discourse; in which case we don't do work translating thoughts into dream images, but the other way round, and condensation is not a process by which latent thoughts are elided into dreams but the state of affairs that exists when the capacity to use language discursively is, as in sleep, in abeyance.

Displacement

Displacement is the term used by Freud to describe the process by which the meaning of something is transferred onto something else, so that the latter stands for, symbolizes, refers to, replaces, alludes to the former. In Freudian theory it is one of the primary processes characteristic of unconscious thinking. In Freud's own theorizing, what is conceived to be displaced is mental energy (libido or cathexis), which is imagined to be withdrawn from one mental image and displaced onto another one, which then becomes a symbolic substitute, equivalent or successor for (of) the former; the analogy being to an electric charge which can move (be moved) from one structural unit (image or object representation) of the mind, itself conceived of as an apparatus, to another. If, however, one drops the mechanical, electrical analogy, what is displaced can be seen to be 'meaning' or 'interest'.

Displacement can be from the whole to a part, from something to something else which resembles it, and from something to something else which is spatially or temporally associated with it. In other words displacement obeys the laws of association and generates figures of speech; displacement from whole to part producing synecdoche, displacement from something to something else which resembles it producing metaphor, and displacement from something to something else associated with it producing metonymy.

An example: a man who was an only child and whose father had deserted home early in his childhood, opened his analysis by telling a dream. He was swimming alone in the sea and saw a large sailing ship bearing down upon him. The ship was in full sail with its mainsails billowing and its bowsprit jutting forwards. He then remarked, without prompting, that of course the ship stood for his mother, the mainsails for her breasts, and the bowsprit for the penis he had always imagined her to have. This dream, then, represents the dreamer's conception of his relationship to his mother by a set of interlocking metaphors. His mother is likened to a ship, large, overbearing, and powerful—being possessed of both maternal and paternal attributes. The dreamer, in contrast, is presented as small (in comparison to both the ship and the sea) and at sea, this last being a dead metaphor borrowed from speech. The representation of his mother as a sailing ship—she was either a tea-clipper or a windjammer—is a live metaphor, since overbearing women are usually spoken of as battleships not as sailing ships. The use of a bowsprit to represent a penis and hence his mother's masculine attributes is synecdoche, the part, the penis, standing for the whole, the father.

Since displacement is the process which underlies symbol-formation and the creation of figures of speech in both language and dreams, it is perhaps appropriate to quote here Aristotle's view of dream interpretation. He held that the best interpreter of dreams is the man who can best grasp similarities, i.e. who is a master of metaphor, which is 'the one thing that cannot be learnt from others'.[12]

The Unconscious and the Id

When Freud postulated that the mind could be likened to an apparatus consisting of two parts or sub-systems, the Conscious (or Ego) and the Unconscious (or Id), each characterized by different modes of thinking, the secondary and primary processes respectively, he had to include the rider that parts of the Conscious could at times be unconscious—i.e. that thoughts belonging to the System Conscious could be descriptively unconscious—and that parts of the Unconscious could at times be conscious—i.e. that parts of the system Unconscious could at times be descriptively conscious—dreams being the prime and most familiar example of the latter. What he meant by this was that, although we are aware while dreaming of what we are dreaming and may on occasion be able to remember our dreams, the mode of thinking exemplified in dreaming is that of the System Unconscious not that of the System Conscious, that the laws governing the construction of dreams are not those governing the construction of waking thoughts, i.e. the arrangement of words sequentially with respect for syntax, logic and the categories of space and time, but something quite different, a set of rules by which images, not words, are fused with one another (condensation), replace one another (displacement), symbolize one another (symbolization) in a context that disregards the categories of space and time. This set of rules Freud designated the primary processes.

I have already described this set of rules in the sections above on the Primary and Secondary Processes, Condensation, and Displacement, where I also gave my reasons for thinking that the differences between the modes of thought of consciousness and dreaming are better described by reference to Susanne Langer's discursive and non-discursive symbolism and that dreaming is better regarded as a variety of imaginative activity than as the intrusion into consciousness of an archaic mode of thinking that is normally repressed. Here I would only emphasize that Freud's concept of the unconscious or id is part and parcel of a mechanistic model of the mind which places various kinds of mental activity in various positions inside a fictive apparatus, whereas the fact of the matter is that we are people who think, imagine, feel and act, sometimes consciously, sometimes unconsciously. What I am suggesting here, and argue at greater length in the section on Action Language, is that concepts like the Unconscious are unnecessary, redundant, scientistic, and hypostasizing—the last since the concept the Unconscious insinuates the idea that there really is some entity somewhere that instigates whatever we do unconsciously, some entity which is not the same entity as instigates whatever we do consciously.

In 1923 Freud[13] renamed the unconscious the 'id'—or, rather, Freud's English translators used 'id', which is the Latin for 'it', to translate his 'das Es' (the 'it'), a term he borrowed from Groddeck. Freud's Id and Groddeck's It do not however mean exactly the same thing, as comparison of the following quotations shows.

According to Groddeck, 'body and mind are one unit that contain an It, a force which lives us while we believe we are living ... The It, which is mysteriously connected with sexuality, with *eros* or whatever you choose to call it, shapes man's nose and hand as well his thoughts and emotions.'[14] In Groddeck's view the It is that by which we are dreamt, it is the agent which sends us messages to which we may or may not listen, which we may or not understand. It is the impersonal self by which our personal, egotistical self is lived.

According to Freud, however, the id 'contains everything that is inherited, that is present at birth, that is laid down in the constitution—above all, therefore, the instincts, which originate from the somatic organization and find a first psychical expression here (i.e. in the id) in forms unknown to us.'[15] In Freud's view, then, the Id is the source of the wishes that seek hallucinatory wish-fulfilment in dreams, but the agent who constructs the dreams is not the id but that part of the mind which converts wishes into disguised symbolic form in order to preserve sleep. In several sections of this book I give reasons for doubting Freud's idea that the aim of dreaming is to preserve sleep and that the process of dream-formation involves the dreamer doing work translating unconscious id-wishes into incomprehensible form, and take up a position much nearer Groddeck's than Freud's.

Manifest and Latent Content · Dream Work

According to classical Freudian theory, the dream as remembered and reported by the dreamer constitutes its manifest content, its latent content being those thoughts, wishes and feelings which provoked the dream and which would, had it not been for their conversion into a dream, have disturbed sleep. In other words, Freud believed that dreams have, as it were, an original text, which encounters censorship, and is redrafted into a form that the dreamer cannot understand; and that the dreamer does work converting the latent into the manifest content.

Dream work, then, is the process by which, according to Freudian theory, the latent content of a dream (i.e. its original, undisguised text) is translated into its manifest content (i.e. the text as actually remembered and reported by the dreamer). According to this view, dreams are specific mental acts, which have only one function, that of preventing the sleeper being awakened by disturbing thoughts and wishes which are present during sleep by converting them into disguised wish-fulfilling hallucinations. Whereas Jung thought it probable that we dream continuously, even while awake, the strict Freudian view is that mental activity occurring during sleep only becomes dreaming if and when it is subjected to the specific process of being converted by the 'dream work' into a dream. This point is made by Jones in a passage in which he is clearly concerned to protect rigorous Freudian thinking from the wooliness of Jungians, mystics and 'the post-psychoanalytical school'.

The dream work is concerned solely with translating into another form various underlying dream thoughts that were previously in existence. No creative work is carried out by the process of dream making; it performs no act of decision, calculation, judgement, comparison, conclusion, or any kind of thought.[16]

For a discussion of the extent to which Freud and Jung were both right and wrong in their view of the relationship between dreaming and sleeping, see the sections on sleep (chapter 6) and on Jung on Dreams (Chapter 2)

Free Association and Secondary Revision

Free association is the technical Freudian term for elucidating the meaning of an image in a dream by discovering the first idea that occurs to the dreamer when he thinks of it and then following on from there to wherever his unfettered train of thoughts leads him—or until he encounters a block to further thought. The rationale behind it is the assumption that the free associations to the various details of a dream will converge on to a common theme, i.e. that, psychologically speaking, all roads lead to Rome, Rome being whatever thought or wish has instigated the dream.

Freud used free association extensively when analysing his own dreams pen in hand and the technique, which involves breaking dreams down into single items instead of apprehending them as a whole, must have played a part in his choice of the term psychoanalysis to describe his form of psychotherapy. The comparable Jungian technique is called amplification (see Chapter 2, p. 36)

Curiously enough, the term is based on a mistranslation by Brill in the first English, or rather American, translation of *The Interpretation of Dreams*. The original German was 'freier Einfall' and 'Einfall' means 'irruption', 'inroad', or 'sudden idea' not association. In other words, the technique of free association involves the subject in taking up a receptive attitude towards whatever ideas emerge or irrupt when he allows himself to stop trying to grasp the meaning of his dream actively and intellectually. The significance of this last sentence will become apparent to the reader when he reaches the early sections of Chapter 3.

Secondary revision, often called, again owing to a mistranslation, secondary elaboration, is on the face of it a very different concept, It refers to the process by which a person telling a dream gives it greater internal consistency and coherence than it in fact had in order to make it comprehensible to whomever he tells it. And since most dreams are expressed in non-verbal, non-discursive imagery, secondary revision cannot be distinguished from the process of translating a dream from pictures into discourse.

But since the person who dreams a dream, the person who associates freely to it, and the person who secondarily revises it, are all the same person, free association and secondary elaboration can be seen to be different facets of the single process by which a dreamer attempts to assimilate his dream into the totality of himself, by which he seeks to establish connections between the discrete figure of his dream and the general background of his self. The significance of *this* last sentence will become apparent to the reader when he reaches the later sections of Chapter 3.

Since free association and secondary revision are techniques which dreamers only use if they want to discover what their dreams mean, they are not, strictly speaking, parts, extensions or elaborations of the dream but parts of the process by which the dreamer tries to arrive at its meaning. But since, again, the Dreamer, the free associator and the secondary reviser are all the same person, to the extent that any dream is understood and its meaning assimilated, it becomes immaterial, and indeed meaningless, to ask whether the free associations and the secondary revisions originate in the dream or in the dreamer;

just as when two people come to understand one another, the precise stages by which they did so, the precise contribution each made to their doing so, ceases to be of any significance. If someone has a dream the meaning of which he is ready to accept, he will describe the dream in words which facilitate understanding and produce associations which lead him directly to it, but if, on the other hand, someone has a dream which he is not ready to understand, both the words he uses to describe it and the associations he produces to it will be chosen to ensure that he does not do so.*

Dreams from Below and Dreams from Above

Although Freud continued throughout his life to subscribe to his own theory of dreams, in the 1920s he made a partial concession to the more common sense idea that dreams are a continuation in sleep of thoughts which were exercising the sleeper while he was awake, by distinguishing between 'dreams from below' and 'dreams from above'.

Dreams from below are those which are provoked by the strength of an unconscious (repressed) wish which has found a means of being represented in some of the day's residues. They may be regarded as inroads of the repressed into waking life. Dreams from above correspond to thoughts or intentions of the day before which have contrived during the

---

* This section will, perhaps, be more comprehensible to those readers who have ever been analysts or analysands than to those who have never put themselves in a position in which they have to take dreams seriously, since they will know by experience that it is neither feasible nor profitable to demarcate clearly dreams as actually dreamt, dreams as recounted in words, and the ideas that occur to the dreamer while he is recounting a dream or reflecting upon it. It is, in any case, inconceivable that one could ever record the pure text of any dream, uncontaminated by the words the dreamer uses to describe it.

night to obtain reinforcement from repressed material that is debarred from the ego.[17]

It should be noted, however, that this formulation continues to give primacy to 'repressed material that is debarred from the ego' and that Freud is not really distinguishing between two different kinds of dreams, but merely stating that imagery and ideas deriving from 'repressed materials' and 'day's residues' may be mixed in differing proportions in different dreams.

'Day's residue' is the technical Freudian term for those elements in a dream which derive from some event, observation, or thought which occurred to the dreamer during the waking period immediately prior to the sleep in which the dream took place. According to Ernest Jones, who was always a more intransigent Freudian than Freud himself ever was, 'In every dream without exception occur mental processes experienced by the subject in the last waking interval . . . the experience in question may be either psychically significant or indifferent; in the latter case, however, it is always associated with some underlying significant experience.'[18] The inference is that dream-formation requires an instigator or trigger event in the dreamer's waking life—this instigator bearing some actual or symbolic relation to a repressed impulse striving for expression.

Freud's Irma dream, which I discuss in the last section of this chapter, is an excellent example of a dream containing elements derived from a psychically significant experience of the previous day.

Regression

In Freud's view dreams were regressive phenomena, the regression occurring during them being of three kinds.

First, he postulated that during dreams there is a backward movement of mental energy.

The only way in which we can describe what happens in hallucinatory dreams is by saying that the excitation moves in a backward direction. Instead of being transmitted towards the *motor* end of the apparatus it moves towards the sensory end and finally reaches the perceptual system.[19]

This idea formed an intrinsic part of Freud's attempt to construct a scientific psychology in which mental phenoma would be explicable in terms of the movement within a 'psychic apparatus' of mental energy, the 'normal' flow of which was from the sensory to the motor end, from stimulus to response. According to such a theory, the fact, if it is one, that we attribute objective reality to our dreams, can only be explained by assuming that during dreaming the sensory part of the apparatus, which includes memories, is retrogressively activated. Elsewhere in, and indeed throughout, this book, I give reasons for doubting whether it is in order to think of mental experiences as phenomena or whether it is possible to attach any meaning to the concept of mental energy.

In later editions of the *Interpretation of Dreams* Freud quotes in a footnote,[20] and in support of his own thesis, a remark of Hobbes's that 'our dreams are the reverse of our waking imaginations, the motion, when we are awake, beginning at one end and when we dream at another'. But his main text shows that Freud did not think that waking imagination moves forwards and dreams move backwards, but that in all imagining energy moves backwards—the movement being, however, further backward in dreams than in any waking imaginative activity, 'producing a hallucinatory revival of the perceptual images'[21], as opposed to the revival of memory images that can occur while awake. I must confess that I find myself floored by the idea of a distinction between backward and forward movements of the imagination.

Secondly, according to Freud, dreams are regressive, because they hark back to the past and are 'a revival of his (the dreamer's) childhood, of the instinctual impulses which dominated him and of the methods of expression which were then available to him.'[22]

And thirdly, dreams display formal regression, 'where primitive methods of expression and representation take the place of the usual ones'.[23] My reasons for doubting whether the methods of expression and representation used in dreams really are as primitive as Freud thought are given elsewhere in this book, notably in the preceding sections on the primary and secondary processes. Here I only need point out that Freud seems to have assumed that in fully awake, 'normal' consciousness ideas and thoughts are not accompanied by imagery, an assumption that made it possible for him to write: 'We call it regression when in a dream an idea is turned back into the sensory image from which it was originally derived.'[24] One can only surmise that for Freud thought was imageless; and even in dreams he would appear to have experienced less imagery than he himself considered usual: 'My dreams are in general less rich in sensory elements than I am led to suppose is the case in other people.'[25]

In fact, the absence of imagery accompanying thought seems to be an idiosyncrasy common among scientists and intellectuals. When Francis Galton circulated a questionnaire on imagery he

found that the great majority of the men of science to whom I first applied protested that mental imagery was unknown to them, and they looked on me as fanciful and fantastic in supposing that the words 'mental imagery' really expressed what I believed everybody supposed them to mean. They had no more notion of its true nature than a colour-blind man, who has not discerned his defect, has of the nature of colour ... On the other hand, when I spoke to persons whom I met in general society, I found an entirely different disposition to prevail. Many men and a yet larger number of women, and many boys and girls, declared that they habitually saw mental imagery, and that it was perfectly distinct to them and full of colour ... My own conclusion is, that an over-ready perception of sharp mental pictures is antagonistic to the acquirement of habits of highly generalised and abstract thought, especially when the steps of reasoning are carried on by words as symbols, and that if the faculty of seeing the pictures was ever possessed by men who think hard, it is very apt to be lost by disuse. The highest minds are probably those in which it is not lost, but subordinated, and is ready for use on suitable occasions.[26]

It seems possible, therefore, that Freud's view of dreams as regressive, primitive, archaic phenomena was determined, in part at least, by his assumption that his own lack of visual imagery was normal and that manifestation of such a faculty must, therefore, of necessity indicate some individual or evolutionary immaturity.

Dreams of the Neurotic and the Healthy

Freud's assumption that dreams are analogous to neurotic symptoms led him to argue that the healthy are virtual neurotics.

But the dreams of neurotics do not differ in any important respect from those of normal people; it is possible, indeed, that they cannot be distinguished from them at all. It would be absurd to give an account of the dreams of neurotics which could not also apply to the dreams of normal people. We must therefore say that the difference between neurosis and health holds only during the day; it is not prolonged into dream-life. We are obliged to carry over to healthy people a number of hypotheses which arise in connection with neurotics as a result of the links between the latter's dreams and their symptoms. We cannot deny that healthy people as well possess in their mental life what alone makes possible the formation both of dreams and of symptoms, and we must conclude that they too have carried out repressions, that they

27

expend a certain amount of energy in order to maintain them, that their unconscious system conceals repressed impulses which are still cathected with energy, and that a portion of their libido is withdrawn from their ego's disposal. Thus a healthy person, too, is virtually a neurotic; but dreams appear to be the only symptoms which he is capable of forming.[27]

In this passage Freud seems to have tied himself in knots in his attempt to have his cake and eat it; he maintains that dreams are symptoms but also that they are universal occurrences; he maintains that the distinction between neurotic and healthy is a real one but that the essential mechanism of neurosis, repression, occurs universally among the healthy; and he implies both that psycho-analysis is a form of treatment for neurotics and that it is applicable to the healthy too. It would, one feels, have been much simpler to argue that the distinction between health and neurosis does not survive psychoanalytical scrutiny, that dreams are not symptoms but normal events which conform to the same rules in everyone regardless of whether they suffer from neurotic symptoms or not, but that dreams offer a special mode of access to understanding the personal conflicts that give rise to neurotic symptoms.

The statement that the dreams of neurotics do not differ 'in any important respect' from those of normal people seems to me to be only formally true, in the sense that there is no reason to suppose that people who develop neurotic symptoms use different processes or 'grammatical' rules when constructing dreams than people who don't. I even doubt whether they exploit the obfuscating and self-deceiving possibilities of symbolism more or less than others. But the dreams of persons who suffer neurotic symptoms certainly differ from those who do not inasmuch as their symptoms are reflected in their dreams; anxious people have anxious dreams, phobic people dream of being in dangerous or safe places, depressive people dream of violence and failures to repair damage, schizoid people dream of remote places and of catastrophes and devastation.

Freud's idea that the difference between neurosis and health holds only during the day and is not prolonged into dream-life strikes me, therefore, as most peculiar. Either, the distinction between them does not hold at all, even during the day, since mechanisms such as repression can be demonstrated in both, or it holds as much in dreams as in waking life, since some dreams, for instance nightmares, are symptoms of which people can complain and for which they can seek treatment.

This passage is, incidentally, a clear example of the logical tangles that can arise if one slides from the statement that people can suffer from neurotic, i.e. psychogenic, symptoms to the assertions that they have a neurosis or, even worse, are neurotics. Freud, however, lived and wrote without benefit of linguistic philosophy.

Freud's Irma Dream

The first dream that Freud 'submitted to a detailed interpretation' was dreamt during the night of July 23rd–24th, 1895. It concerns a young widow—Freud calls her Irma—who was both a patient of Freud's and a friend of the family. The previous day a colleague and friend of Freud, Otto, who had been staying with Irma and her family at their country resort, had mentioned to Freud that Irma was 'better, but not quite well'. Freud detected a note of reproof in this remark and, in a mood of self-justification, spent the evening writing out her case-history. That night he had a long dream—the English translation runs to 28 lines of print—in which Irma attends a reception given by the Freuds, is reproached by Freud for not accepting his 'solution', and complains bitterly of pains in her throat, stomach and abdomen. Freud then looks into her mouth, discovers a large white patch and 'some remarkable curly structures which were evidently modelled on the turbinal bones of the nose'. Freud then calls in Dr M, who repeats the examination and confirms it, and two other doctors, 'my friend Otto' and 'my friend Leopold' appear on the scene. Dr M diagnoses an infection and then 'we' become 'directly aware of the origin of the infection'. 'My friend Otto' had given her an injection of propionic acid trimethalin and probably the syringe had not been clean.[28]

Freud noted down the dream immediately after awakening and then, some unspecified time later, he undertook 'a detailed analysis', writing down his 'free associations' to specific items of the text of the dream. Freud's report of this analysis occupies fourteen pages of his *The Interpretation of Dreams*.[29] And while he was writing it, the meaning of the dream became apparent to him:

> ... in the meantime the 'meaning' of the dream was borne in upon me. I became aware of an intention which was carried into effect by the dream and which must have been my motive for dreaming it. The dream fulfilled certain wishes which were started in me by the events of the previous evening. The conclusion of the dream, that is to say, was that I was not responsible for the persistence of Irma's pains but that Otto was. Otto had in fact annoyed me by his remarks about Irma's incomplete cure, and the dream gave me my revenge by throwing the reproach back on him. The dream acquitted me of the responsibility for Irma's condition by showing that it was due to other factors—it produced a whole series of reasons. The dream represented a particular state of affairs as I should have wished it to be. Thus its content was the fulfilment of a wish and its motive was a wish.'[30]

Freud writes as though this dream and its interpretation was a revelation and a turning-point in his life. In 1900, indeed, he allowed himself the fantasy that one day a marble tablet would be placed on the house in which he dreamt it, saying 'In This House on July 24th, 1895, the Secret of Dreams was Revealed to Dr Sigm. Freud.'

And yet, today and with hindsight, it is the omissions that strike one. The wish that is represented as fulfilled, that Irma's symptoms are not his fault but Otto's, is not an instinctual one, still less a sexual or an infantile one, but one deriving from professional conscientiousness and pride; symbolism is not invoked; and the characters appearing in the dream are all assumed to represent themselves and not to stand for others or for parts of Freud's own self.

In view of the importance Freud attached to this dream and of the place it occupies in the history of psychoanalysis—and in view too of the infinite scope it offers for speculation; could Freud, one wonders, have found Irma attractive and been jealous of Otto, who had just spent a week-end with her?—it is hardly surprising that an extensive literature has grown up about it and that it has acquired a title: the dream specimen of psychoanalysis. A recent paper by Mahoney even offers sexual interpretations of Freud's inconsistent use of dashes, ellipses and parentheses in the original German text. A fact mentioned by Mahoney but not by Freud is that at the time of the dream Frau Freud was in her sixth pregnancy.[31]

CHAPTER 2

Jung's View of Dreams

Introductory

Jung seems, from the very beginning, to have regarded dreams as creations, as messages from an agent, though he seems also to have had some difficulty in deciding who or what this agent is —or, perhaps better, in finding a satisfactory term for naming him or it. Hence such statements as 'The dream is a mysterious message from our night-aspect'[1] and 'One does not dream: one is dreamed. We "undergo" the dream, we are the objects.'[2] The latter formulation leaves the subject, the dreamer who composes the message, unnamed.

According to Jolande Jacobi the fundamental difference between Jungian and other analytical theories of dreams is that the Jungian regards dreams as manifestations and creations of not only the Personal but also the Collective Unconscious. So in the Jungian view the agent who sends messages in dreams is both the personally impersonal part of oneself—what Freud, following Groddeck, called the Id or It—and the collectively impersonal part of oneself, which one shares with others.

Jung seems also to have believed that we continually dream even while awake. 'It is on the whole probable that we continually dream, but that consciousness makes such a noise that we do not hear it.'[3] This statement implies that Jung did not distinguish between dreaming and what Freudians call 'unconscious phantasy', and that he rejected Freud's view that dreams are specific events and constructions, the function of which is to preserve sleep by granting the dreamer disguised hallucinatory fulfilment of wishes which would otherwise wake him up. As a result Jungian theory has no concept of dream work and does not assume that the function of symbolism in dreams is to disguise the nature of the wishes being expressed in them. 'There is no reason under the sun why we should assume that the dream is a crafty device to lead us astray.'[4]

In the event both Freud and Jung seem to have been partly right, partly wrong. Laboratory research (see Chapter 6) on the physiology of dreaming suggests that dreams are specific events and that we do not dream continually, even during sleep, but does not support Freud's idea that we dream in order not to wake up; it suggests rather that dreaming is a phasic activity and that one of the reasons why we sleep is in order to dream, and that the function of dreaming has more to do with integration and making psycho-physical rearrangements than with hallucinatory gratification of repressed wishes. And the evidence provided by dreams reported by people not in analytical treatment suggests that symbolization in dreams does not occur in order to conceal the nature of inadmissible wishes —the same dreamer may express the same idea directly and symbolically in successive dreams.[5]

The Collective Unconscious

This Jungian concept postulates a part or layer of the mind which is common to all men and which is responsible for producing dreams, myths, visions and religious ideas. The concept seeks to explain why the dreams and delusions of Western man may resemble the myths and religious ideas of cultures with which the Western dreamer or psychotic is personally unfamiliar.

The concept, which came to Jung in a dream quoted later in this book (see p. 91), seems to be capable of two interpretations; first, that there is indeed some sort of group mind, parts of which may be located within or under the personal minds of individuals; and secondly, that 'the fundamental and perennial interests of mankind', to quote a phrase of Jones's are so uniform that persons of different cultures may spontaneously and independently create identical symbolic imagery, the likelihood of this happening being increased by the fact that human bodies and biological functions are everywhere similar and that, therefore, metaphors based on body symbolism, i.e. on resemblances between objects external to the self and bodily parts and functions, are likely to be universally comprehensible.

If what I argue in the sections on Action Language and on the Unconscious is correct, the issue is not whether there is a Collective Unconscious as well as a personal Unconscious, but whether it makes any sense to divide actions and thoughts that we perform unconsciously into some that we perform personally unconsciously and others that we perform collectively unconsciously. When we act unconsciously, it is we ourselves who are unconscious of the act we performed, but it is not at all clear who is or should be regarded as unconscious of acts performed collectively unconsciously. The circumstances under which Jung had the dream which led him to 'discover' the collective unconscious, strongly suggest that he was concerned at the time to liberate himself from Freud's influence and to establish a territory of his own.[6]

Persona and Shadow

The term 'persona' was used by Jung to describe the mask or demeanour which people adopt to deal with the requirements of everyday life. According to Jung, people who identify excessively with their persona are apt to have dreams in which a person conspicuously unlike their persona appears, this other 'opposite' person being the dreamer's 'shadow'. As an example of persona and shadow, Bennet[7] cites a punctilious bank official who recurrently dreamt that while looking up at night he became aware of a figure trying to break into his house. This figure would move from window to window, each of which he closed in the nick of time, but eventually the intruder outstripped him, burst in through a door—at which point the dreamer woke with a start. The implication is that the intruder represented all that the bank official had disowned of himself.

Plato, one imagines, would have approved the concepts of persona and shadow. 'In all of us, even in good men, there is a lawless wild beast nature which peers out in sleep.'[8]

Initial Dreams

'Initial dream' is a Jungian term referring to a dream recounted by a patient at the onset of treatment and often provoked by the prospect of starting treatment. 'It frequently happens at the very beginning of treatment that a dream will reveal to the doctor, in broad perspective, the whole programme of the unconscious.'[9] Freudian analysts are also taught to pay particular attention to the first dream their patients tell them. As an example of an initial dream, Bennet[10] cites a woman who dreamt, the night before her first interview with him, that she was alone in a stockaded enclosure set in a tropical forest; outside were a variety of wild animals, including a lion, a tiger, and a hippopotamus, watching her. Bennet drew the rather obvious conclusion that this woman was frightened of her instincts, represented by the wild animals, and had had to exclude them. Rather similarly, a patient of mine dreamt the image of a bird in a cage: it emerged that, like a bird in a cage, she could sing beautifully but do nothing else, and that her mother had been a barmaid throughout her childhood. Cage bars, public house bars and musical bars combined to form a cluster of images capable of being used to express ideas about expressive activity and their inhibition and control. I should, however, be guilty of being wise after the event if I pretended that my patient's initial dream revealed more to me when I first heard it than that she felt inhibited; only when I appreciated how musical she was, did I realize that her dilemma was that she could sing but not fly.

35

Anticipatory Dreams

Jung used this term to describe dreams in which something appears to happen that does in fact later happen. Anticipatory dreams may give the impression of being prophetic, but are in fact evidence that while asleep, as while awake, we may envisage the possible outcomes of things we are concerned about, and that of the various possibilities we envisage, one may be what actually happens. 'But just as our conscious thoughts often occupy themselves with the future and its possibilities, so do the unconscious and its dreams.'[11] Anticipatory dreams '. . . are no more prophetic than a medical diagnosis or a weather forecast. They are merely an anticipatory combination of probabilities which may coincide with the actual behaviour of things but need not necessarily agree in every detail.'[12]*

Amplification and Active Imagination

This is a technique of dream interpretation used by Jungians. The dreamer is asked to amplify on the dream, to give his impressions of it, to say what strikes him particularly about it. It plays a role analogous to that played in Freudian analysis by free association. Amplification, in the extended sense of asking the dreamer to make up additions to the dream, would presumably be Active Imagination. This is a Jungian therapeutic technique of encouraging patients to enter, while awake, into a frame of mind analogous to dreaming in which 'images have a life of their own' and 'symbolic events develop according to their own logic—that is, of course, if your conscious reason does not interfere.'[13] Bennet likens this frame of mind to a 'brown study' and argues, following Jung, that we can train ourselves to induce it and thereby contact the uncon-

* Prophetic dreams, i.e. dreams which declared future events that the dreamer did not envisage and could not have envisaged, would, if they occurred, be precognitive phenomena.

scious while still awake and conscious. Both Bennet and Jung are careful to distinguish active imagination from 'fantasy' in the sense of day-dreaming, which is our 'own invention and remains on the surface of personal things and conscious expectations.' Bennet and Jung are, I think, making the same distinction as Coleridge made between Imagination and Fancy, the former being the activity—if that is the right word—of allowing familiar images to dissolve and fuse to create new ones, the latter being that of reassembling images already constituted.

CHAPTER 3

Imagination, Dreaming and the Self

Imagination

The *Shorter Oxford English Dictionary* lists three non-obsolete definitions of the word 'imagination', all of which are applicable to dreams. First, imagination is 'the action of imagining, or forming a mental concept of what is not actually present to the senses'. Secondly, it is 'that faculty of the mind by which we conceive the absent as if it were present'. And thirdly, it is 'the power which the mind has of forming concepts beyond those derived from external objects'.

Dreaming is, accordingly, an imaginative activity since, first, it forms mental images of what is not actually present to the senses, secondly, it conceives such images as though they were present, and thirdly, it forms concepts beyond those derived from external objects. Two qualifications need, however, to be made to the statement that dreaming and indeed imaginative activity in general forms concepts 'beyond those' derived from external objects. First, the clinical evidence in respect of dreams and the literary evidence in respect of poetic imagination suggests that the apparently novel images appearing in dreams and poems are not created out of nothing, are not conjured out of nowhere, but are produced by the fragmentation of images derived from external objects and recombination of the resulting fragments. Freud called this process condensation and Coleridge called it secondary imagination,* which 'dissolves, diffuses, dissipates, in order to recreate'.[1]

---

* Primary imagination being the process by which the mind creates percepts and images out of sensations.

38

Secondly, the clinical evidence suggests that the 'external objects' of which concepts and images are formed during dreaming include the dreamer's own body and parts of it.

Recognition of the fact that dreaming is imaginative activity occurring during sleep and is not, as Freud argued, a symptom analogous to the hallucinations of the insane or the conversion-symptoms of hysterics, is both liberating and simplifying. It allows a universally occurring experience—or a universally experienced occurrence—to be regarded as healthy and normal and not as, in principle, pathological; and it obviates the need to argue, as Freud did,[2] that the healthy are virtual neurotics and that the imaginative and creative are actual neurotics. And, as I have already mentioned, Freud expended much ink and energy trying to prove that artists are neurotics, only reluctantly abandoning the attempt when in 1928 he wrote: 'Before the problem of the creative artist analysis must, alas, lay down its arms.' But, I am suggesting, the creative artist only constituted for him a problem, which had alas to be abandoned, because he had started by assuming that dreams are symptoms and that waking imaginative activity resembles dreaming and must, therefore, also be a symptom. Things would have been much easier for him and his followers if he had made the opposite assumption, viz. that imagination is a normal, universal function or faculty, that dreaming is its sleeping form, and that, if people have neurotic conflicts, these will manifest themselves in their dreams and their waking imaginative products.

Although dictionaries do not mention the fact, imaginative activity, waking or sleeping, is independent of the will. Awake we can make ourselves do things or make ourselves think about things, but we can only let ourselves imagine and may be surprised by what we find ourselves imagining. Asleep we cannot make ourselves do anything, even dream; we just do dream, and even the most experienced analysand or analyst continues to be surprised by his dreams.

This point was well made by Darwin, who wrote:

The Imagination is one of the highest prerogatives of man. By this faculty he unites former images and ideas, independently of the will, and thus creates brilliant and novel results. A poet, as Jean Paul Richter remarks, 'who must reflect whether he shall make a character say yes or no—to the devil with him; he is only a stupid corpse'. Dreaming gives us the best notion of this power; as Jean Paul again says, 'The dream is an involuntary kind of poetry.'[3]*

All dreams must be deemed imaginative in the sense that they consist of images of what is not present conceived as though they were present and are created independently of the will. But some, perhaps even most, dreams are fanciful rather than imaginative in as much as they consist of images and units of meaning which already form part of the furniture of the dreamer's mind without the creation of any new images or meaning. Coleridge's view was that Imagination re-creates in order to say something new, while Fancy is 'no other than a mode of memory emancipated from the order of time and space' and 'must receive all its materials ready made from the law of association.'[4] According to this distinction, only those dreams which express meanings that are to the dreamer novel, in imagery that is to the dreamer surprising, would be deemed imaginative, while those in which the dreamer uses familiar imagery to express familiar meanings would be deemed fanciful. When, for example, a man named Frank dreamt the single word Ernest to remind himself of the importance of being frank, he was, I think, being fanciful not imaginative, since he constructed his dream out of the small change of literary allusion. And when a sluggard dreamt that the grass was growing under his feet, he too was being fanciful since his dream was built on a dead metaphor.

But just as literary critics find it easier to define in general terms the difference between the truly imaginative and the

* In fact, Darwin's text reads 'art of poetry', but 'art' must, I think, be a mistranslation of the German 'Art', meaning 'kind'.

merely fanciful and contrived than to decide whether any particular poem should be labelled one or the other, so dream critics may find it easier to define the difference between imaginative and fanciful dreams—or between 'big' and 'small' dreams (Jung), dreams from above and from below (Freud)—than to decide which particular dream is which.

Dreams

According to the *Shorter Oxford English Dictionary* a dream is 'a train of thoughts, images, or fancies passing through the mind during sleep', and to dream is 'to have visions and imaginary sense-impressions in sleep'.

True dreams differ, therefore, from day-dreams, reveries, castles in the air, etc., in occurring, by definition, during sleep and in being experienced as though they were sensations, without any awareness, while they are occurring, that they are being made up by the dreamer himself as he goes along—the *Shorter Oxford English Dictionary* mentions the suggestion made by Kluge that the word 'dream' is connected with German roots meaning 'to deceive'. It is only on waking reflection that they are recognized as products or creations of ones' own mind—that is, by modern Western secular man, who is not inclined to take seriously the idea that they could be products or creations of someone else's mind.

The one apparent exception to this statement is the interpolated thought 'It's only a dream' which may occur during very frightening dreams. When this happens, the dreamer has, I think, succeeded in seeing through the deception that the dream is really happening without, however, proceeding to the recognition that he has himself been conjuring up the images that have been frightening him.

It would appear that a dreamer may represent to himself as though they were actually happening—he were actually performing them—all bodily actions of which he is or ever was

41

capable*—and all bodily actions of which he can or could ever, while awake, imagine himself capable—undeterred by the limitations imposed by space, time, gravity and the solidity of objects†; that he may experience the whole gamut of emotions, feelings and sensations of which human beings are capable; and that he may be oblivious of incongruities which would strike him immediately if he made up the dream while awake, and which indeed do strike him immediately if he reflects upon it after awakening.

For most people the imagery in dreams is predominantly visual but not exclusively so. Blind people who have never been sighted dream. Musical people may dream music; for instance, a counter-tenor dreamt a flute concerto in which the part for the flute was being played on a clarinet. Dreams of a voice telling the dreamer to wake up seem to be common.

This is about as much as can be said about dreams without qualifications and without recourse to inference and theorizing. It can be inferred from the physiological evidence arising from dream laboratories that everyone dreams every night, but some people sincerely deny ever having done so and everyone remembers fewer dreams than the dream researchers say they have. It can be inferred from clinical evidence and from the text of some dreams that dreams may have meaning, but not even the most enthusiastic dream-interpreter claims to be able to discover meaning in every dream. Those who assert that dreams have meaning have indeed no need to assert that every dream has meaning; the universally accepted idea that waking thoughts can have meaning does not imply that they can

* Paraplegics lacking all sensations in the lower half of their body can dream of performing sexual intercourse culminating in orgasm, blind people who have been sighted can see in dreams for over a decade after losing their sight.[5]

† E.g. dreams of flying, of passing through impassable obstructions, of being in another century, of talking to people known, even during the dream, to be dead, of being in places where one has never been.

never be botched, rubbishy and nonsensical, nor that every meaningful thought is profoundly significant.

Under experimental conditions it can even be inferred that someone *is* dreaming, but the evidence that the inference is correct depends on awakening the sleeper and asking him whether he *was* dreaming. All the information we have about the psychology of dreaming derives from the fact that people can on occasion remember that they have dreamt. We cannot give running commentaries on our dreams as we have them, nor can we act as participant observers in other people's dreams. Nor can we engage in oscillations between dreaming and self-scrutiny as we can when engaged in waking imaginative activity. This fact that we have to stop dreaming and wake up before we can reflect upon what we have dreamt or report our dream to someone else is responsible for the impression of having been in another world that attaches to dreams—and for the fact that, even if, as J. P. Richter said, 'dreams are an involuntary kind of poetry', they often give the impression of being first drafts rather than completed works. Reflective self-awareness has played no part in their composition.

If viewed from the natural scientific point of view, dreams are phenomena; if viewed from the point of view of the humanities, they are activities we engage in, something we do. But if they are designated phenomena, it has to be added that they are phenomena which can only be reported and never observed, and differ from those usually studied by scientists in being subjective not objective. And if they are designated activities or actions, it has to be added that they are actions independent of the will and, furthermore, that they differ from the unwilled imaginative activities of waking life, i.e. those in which we use Keats's negative capability, in that we do not even know, while dreaming, that we are allowing our negative capability to operate. Dreams are then inherently paradoxical experiences which cut across our received categories, since they appear to be phenomena and sensations but have to be subcategorized as subjective, and at the same time appear to be activities analogous to thinking and imagining but have to be described as involuntary, unwilled, self-aware and innocent or unknowing—the last because we do not know what we are about even *while* we are dreaming.

Hallucinations resemble dreams in being forms of mental activity which are experienced as though they were phenomena external to the person who is in fact constructing them. They differ from them in that, by dictionary definition, hallucinations occur while awake and dreams occur while asleep. There seems to be a tendency to classify images occurring while falling asleep (hypnagogic phenomena) and while awakening (hypnopompic phenomena) as hallucinations, even though they are best regarded as transitional states.

Contemporary psychiatry categorizes hallucinations as a symptom, on the ground that a person hallucinating has lost his capacity for reality-testing, and there is a tendency to assume that they are a sign of madness or major psychosis. This is not so. They also occur in childhood, with high fever, in extreme exhaustion, in brain disease, under the influence of drugs including LSD and other psychedelic agents, and during bereavement. And in other cultures, and in our own prior to the scientific revolution, hallucinations have been regarded not as symptoms but as visions with religious, supernatural meaning.

Freud's theory of dreams is based on the assumption that dreams resemble hallucinations and that hallucinations are symptoms. Psychoanalysis would have developed very differently if Freud had assumed, as Jung seems to have, that dreams and hallucinations resemble one another not in their immunity to reality-testing but in their common resemblance to waking imagination.

Meaning

If dreaming is an imaginative activity, dreams must mean something. That being so, there must be a subject, an agent, who is engaged during dreaming in the activity of intending or conveying meaning. This subject or agent can only, unless one takes seriously the possibility of supernatural or telepathic interventions, be (some aspect of) the dreaming sleeper himself, and the dream he constructs must be a message; in which case there must be an indirect object, a recipient, for whom the dream-message is intended and who can be imagined capable of receiving the message and understanding the sense being conveyed to him.

In other words, dreamers must dream for or to someone, and that someone can only be the dreamer himself. It is only in psychotherapeutic relationships and in cultures that employ dream-interpreters as diviners that people dream with the intention of telling their dreams to someone else.

Dreaming is thus a form of communicating or communing with oneself and is analogous to such waking activities as talking to oneself, reminding oneself, exhorting oneself, consoling oneself, frightening oneself, entertaining oneself or exciting oneself with one's own imagination—and, perhaps more particularly, to such waking meditative imaginative activities as summoning up remembrance of things past or envisaging the prospect of things future.

Put another way, dreaming is a special case of reflexive mental activity, in which the self becomes twofold, one part observing, arguing with, reflecting upon, resisting the implications of, assenting to, ideas, thoughts, situations imaginatively presented to it by the other; the speciality of the case deriving from two features of sleep. First, during sleep the body is immobilized and dreamers can, therefore, present to themselves wishes and situations in the certainty that they will not immediately act upon them. It appears, indeed, that most, perhaps all, dreams occur in the so-called paradoxical phase of sleep, during which the body is at one and the same time restless and maximally immobilized and the sleeper hard to arouse. And secondly, during sleep it is the higher, cortical functions that are most asleep, and as a result dreamers present their imaginings to themselves not in the discursive language they use to convey meanings to others but in non-discursive symbolism.

In other words, dreamers, since they are asleep and communing with themselves, do not, as waking talkers do, convey meaning by finding words with an agreed meaning and uttering them in the right order, but instead by conjuring up evocative imagery and relating the particular images evoked to one another spatially as well as temporally. As a result dreams tend to resemble moving pictures more than they resemble literary texts.

Since dreaming is private, reflexive self-to-self communing, the imagery used in dreams need only have private evocative meaning, and the dreamer does not have to make concessions to the fact that no two people ever share an exactly identical store of significant images. As a result he can dispense with language and the lexical and grammatical rules which enable people to communicate with one another despite differences in their experiences and visions of reality (i.e. despite differences in their cognitive, apperceptive world-schemata, or in Coleridgean terminology, primary imagination), and can instead use his own private iconography. In other words, he can use images to refer or allude to ideas, recollections and feelings without being concerned as to whether the references and allusions would be comprehensible to anyone other than himself. Dreamers, unlike poets and, indeed, unlike waking speakers of prose, are not concerned to universalize private meanings.

For instance, a man who had been feeling somewhat discouraged about his career dreamt that another man was drawing his attention to some coats of arms on a wall. After awakening, he remembered that coats of arms can be called 'hatchments' and that 'hatchment' and 'achievement' are etymologically the same word. Now, if he had wanted to encourage someone else, he would not have said to him 'Look at your coats of arms', but knowing as he did that the now entirely abstract noun 'achievement' once had a concrete, visualizable meaning, he could use the heraldic image of an 'achievement' to remind himself of past achievements.

I have cited this dream not only because it is an example of how a thought which in waking language requires a sentence containing an abstract noun can be represented pictorially in a dream, using an image that would not be universally comprehensible, but also because it was a dream which the dreamer had no difficulty in understanding himself—after he had woken up. If all dreams were like this one, in which the recipient had no difficulty in getting the sense of the message conveyed to him by the dreaming agent, there would be no mystery about dreaming; it would be universally agreed that dreams have meaning, and the interpretation of dreams would amount to nothing more than the translation of non-discursive, pictorial statements into words arranged into sentences.

But in fact most dreams are not readily understood by their initial recipient, and the proposition that dreams have meaning is open to the obvious objection that the experiencer of dreams usually fails to register the meaning of the message which—so the proposition asserts—the dream is conveying, or indeed even to register that any message is being conveyed. The idea that, while asleep, we send ourselves significant messages which we either fail to register—as in the case of dreams we fail to remember—or fail to understand, is on the face of it absurd, and anyone maintaining that dreams have meanings has to explain why the recipient of dream-messages commonly does not even listen to them, let alone take heed of them. He has, in other words, to give plausible reasons for supposing that dreams tend to contain unwelcome or disturbing messages to which most people react, much as they do to unwelcome truths about themselves heard while they are awake, that is by ignoring, forgetting or distorting them.

The proposition that dreams have meaning has then to be supported by the subsidiary hypothesis that the meaning conveyed by them tends to be of a kind that the sleeping and later waking recipient is reluctant to understand, and that therefore the division of the self into two parts that occurs during dreaming tends to be such that the agent who constructs dreams tends to possess insights into the person's true nature which the recipient, i.e. the person's waking self, is reluctant to acquire.

This hypothesis presupposes that people tend to be, to a greater or lesser extent, out of touch with their whole selves and are, therefore, predisposed to dismiss as meaningless nonsense messages which, if granted meaning, would compel them to alter and widen their conception of themselves. This in turn presupposes that as people grow up and become increasingly self-aware, they at the same time lose touch with certain aspects of themselves, and that as they acquire a self-conscious conception of themselves as a certain type of person, they engage in self-deceptions, creating a self-image or sense of identity which is incomplete and distorted and can only be preserved by learning the art of not listening to their own true voice.

The meanings conveyed by dreams tend therefore to be rejected by the waking self because they emanate from a total self which still knows what the habitual waking self has forgotten, disowned and repressed. The assumption that dreams have meaning implies in fact that the agent or agency who composes dreams has more self-knowledge and is more honest than the recipient who registers and remembers them.

The same point can be made in another way if one allows oneself to formulate positively Freud's statement that dreams are oblivious of the categories of space and time. It then becomes possible to say that the dreaming self utters meanings from a timeless, total position *sub specie aeternitatis*, while the part of the self that receives dream-messages occupies a pre-empted, prescribed position localized in a particular time and place and possesses a preconceived notion of itself which is at risk if it listens seriously to dream-meanings.

I should perhaps end this section by stating explicitly that I am well aware that the way in which I have sought to reconcile the idea that dreams have meaning with the fact that the majority of dreams are not understood or even granted meaning implies that we live in a culture in which alienation and unconscious hypocrisy are endemic. This assumption is, I think, so widely accepted as not to require arguing.

Interpretation

Given that dreams, despite often appearing to be meaningless, do nonetheless have meaning, it must be possible to interpret them. It must be possible, in other words, to discover the sense they are conveying and to formulate this sense in words. But since dreams, if they are communications, must be communications from one aspect of a person to another aspect of that same person, the criteria for deciding whether any proposed interpretation is in fact the true one differ in quality from those available for deciding whether communications between people have been correctly interpreted.

If we wish to decide whether we have correctly interpreted the meaning of a passage in a book we have been reading, of a lecture we have been listening to, of a text in a foreign language we have been translating, we can check our own interpretation with publically available evidence contained in dictionaries, grammars and reference books, and with the responses of others who have read the same book, who attended the same lecture, who are familiar with the foreign language we are translating. We can, in fact, calibrate and if necessary correct our own provisional interpretation by reference to a public consensus, which exists because everyone within the same cultural, linguistic group agrees more or less on the meaning of the words and syntax used in social utterances.

As a result, the communications we make to, and receive from, others possess a universal or public meaning, which may, on occasion, be ambiguous but is never arbitrary. This is true even of the highly allusive, elliptical and emotionally charged interchanges that occur between intimates, since they too can be checked by cross-reference; we can ask the other whether he (or she) really did intend all the meanings we read into what he said or whether he got the full implications of what we said.

But with the interpretation of dreams things are entirely different. We cannot assume that the imagery used by the dreamer carries the same meaning as it would if it occurred as a word in public discourse, and we cannot ask the dreamer to enlarge on or explain more clearly what it was he intended to indicate—even though we can ask him for information about the context in which he dreamt the dream, i.e. when and under what circumstances he dreamt it and what the imagery in it reminds him of.

As a result, when confronted by a dream, we either have to dismiss it as meaningless or, if we are inclined to ascribe meaning to it and wish to discover what that meaning is, we have to proceed indirectly. And if the dream is one that we have ourselves dreamt, we can either try to discover it for ourselves or enlist the aid of a professional dream interpreter.

If we try to discover it for ourselves, we can proceed in one or other of two apparently opposed ways, one negative, passive and intuitive, the other positive, active and intellectual. But, as we shall see, these two ways ultimately converge.

The negative, intuitive method of interpreting a dream of our own consists in contemplating the dream as a whole, while allowing oneself to enter the state that Keats called 'negative capability, that is, when a man is capable of being in uncertainties, mysteries, doubts, without any irritable reaching after fact and reason[6]'; and then waiting in the hope that a, or the, meaning will emerge. In the section on meaning I quoted a dream in which the dreamer was shown a coat of arms on a wall. He arrived at its meaning by discovering that, as he meditated on the dream, he found himself locating the wall in Canterbury Cathedral and then remembering that it was there that he had first seen the word 'achievement' used on a tomb in its concrete, heraldic sense—and at that moment the dream's meaning occurred to him as a self-evident truth. The whole process of interpretation was passive, unwilled and negative; and the conviction that the interpretation was true was intuitive—it just clicked. And since the sleeping dream and the waking interpretation of it were both self-communing processes, there was no need at any point to refer to any public consensus as to the meaning of the images contained in it, and no need to prove the correctness of its interpretation to anyone else.

If, on the other hand, we decide to adopt the positive, intellectual method, we have to treat the dream we wish to interpret as though it were not a subjective experience of our own but an objective phenomenon—or, better, a text analogous to a passage in a foreign language which we wish to translate. In other words, we treat the dream as though it were someone else's and proceed much as we imagine a psychoanalyst would if we were one of his patients, asking ourselves for associations to its details and deploying experimentally any knowledge of symbolism we may have. But at some point we will be forced back into the realization that it is our own dream and no-one else's, either by recognizing that we are stuck and have some resistance against proceeding further or by realizing that we have arrived at its meaning; at which moment the exercise ceases to be an active and intellectual one and becomes instead passive and intuitive, our conviction of having arrived at the dream's meaning being again independent of whether we could convince anyone else of its truth.

It is unnecessary for me to spell out here what happens if we enlist the help of a professional dream interpreter since this is the mirror-image of how psychoanalysts set about interpreting their patients' dreams, and a general idea of how they do so will, I hope, emerge from other sections of this book, notably those on meaning, symbolism and Freudian and Jungian concepts. But two further points need to be made now. First, psychoanalysts and psychotherapists do not engage in dream interpretation for its own sake; it is always a means to an end, that end being therapeutic, and as a result they are inevitably and correctly more interested in the obstacles patients put up to understanding their dreams, the resistances they display against their meaning, than in the natural understanding they may possess, which can after all take care of itself. And secondly, interpreting the dreams of patients demands of the analyst an ability to use both of the methods I have described above, an ability to oscillate between being negative, passive and intuitive on the one hand and positive, active, and intellectual on the other. Although the analyst may on occasion have to work hard at understanding the defences and symbolic disguises his patients use to conceal the meaning of their dreams, the best, that is the most illuminating and helpful, interpretations tend to come unexpectedly, surprising the analyst as much as they do the patient.[7]

Dreams as Communications

If dreams have meaning, as is being assumed throughout this book, they must be communications from one entity or agency to another. In psychotherapy, it is often assumed that they are communications from the patient to the therapist, often to the extent that the therapist also assumes that they are communications about him, i.e. that all dreams are amenable to transference interpretation. Lovers and friends who tell one another their dreams are using dreams as communications, though here it is often a case of the medium being itself the message, since the point of the exchange is as much the sense of intimacy induced by the sharing of dreams as the conveying of any particular insight, information or feeling.

However, although psychotherapists may have good pragmatic reasons for treating their patients' dreams as though they were communications to themselves, and lovers may have good emotional reasons for sharing their dreams, the idea that dreaming is a form of inter-personal communication is not seriously tenable. Dreaming occurs when we are subjectively if not objectively alone; everyone dreams but only a few people have psychotherapists to tell them to, the majority of dreams are

forgotten before the awakened dreamer can have any opportunity to tell them to anyone; many dreams are so unpleasant
or peculiar or complicated that their dreamer has to overcome
reluctance to tell them even when he has a therapeutic or
scientific reason for doing so. Only in cultures like the Senoi,
the Malayan tribe in which the telling and interpreting of
dreams is part of the breakfast routine,[8] do people ever recount
dreams as a matter of course. Elsewhere dreams are only
recounted for some special reason; because one is in psychotherapy, because one is participating in a scientific experiment,
because one is consulting an augur, soothsayer or oneiromancer,
or because there seems to be something special about the
dream which justifies telling it to someone else, e.g. because
one is uncertain as to whether it was a dream or not, because it
appears to refer to some event one could not have known about,
or because it strikes one as entertainingly absurd or funny. In
these last cases one is, however, not recounting the dream as a
dream for its own sake but because it is a possible real event, or
a possible telepathic experience, or because it can be told as a
joke.

So dreams must be communications not between two persons but between two aspects of the same person; they must, as
contemporary jargon has it, be intra-personal not inter-personal communications. As Jung said, 'the dream is a mysterious
message from our night-aspect', and according to Calvin Hall,
'A dream is a personal document, a letter to oneself. It is not a
newspaper story or a magazine article.'[9] Both these statements
emphasize the essentially private nature of dreaming, but
neither helps much when it comes to defining the difference
between the self who dreams dreams and the self who receives
dreams and on occasion remembers them. Classical Freudian
psychoanalysis side-stepped this problem by objectifying
dreams, by treating them as hallucination-like mental phenomena which did not require an agent who constructed them,
since they were mental events that happened to, that were
perceived by, people when they were alseep. According to this

view, the self refers only to the waking self, the conscious self, dreaming is an impersonal activity of an impersonal structure, the unconscious or id, and the question of communication or messages does not arise. If, however, one rejects, as I do, the idea that mental activity is a series of events that happen to people and insists instead that all thinking and all imaginative activity implies some agent who creates them, then dreams imply the existence not only of a person or self who has them and remembers them but also of a self, a person, an active dreamer, who dreams them. But this active dreamer proves to be a difficult fellow to pin down, since one seems to get involved in verbal paradox when trying to describe him; he seems to be part of oneself and yet at the same time more than oneself, to be one's true self and yet impersonal, and he sends messages to one's 'day aspect' not because he wills to do so but because he cannot do otherwise.

Dreams as Sources of Information

When we talk—or write—we convey more information to our audience than just the specific, intended meaning of the sentence we have uttered. This is because our accent, our style, our vocabulary and syntax, our use or misuse of metaphor and allusion, our precision or vagueness of expression, reveal aspects of ourselves over and above our wish to convey some particular meaning; while speaking we unwittingly, though not necessarily unwillingly, reveal information about our social class, education, and intelligence and also, in all but the briefest utterances, information about our habits of thought, our values, prejudices and preconceptions. Indeed we even, as a series of papers by Cobb and Lorenz[10] has shown, betray our psychiatric diagnosis—if we use the word 'it' frequently and vaguely, we are probably hysterical; if we habitually construct sentences in two opposed parts joined by a 'but', we are probably obsessional; if we scramble syntax, or consistently fail to reveal whether we are talking literally or metaphorically, we are probably schizoid.

It seems, in fact, that it is impossible for an agent to utter meaningful statements without at the same time revealing information about himself—or his Self—his biography, personality and character. Even the apparent obvious exception turns out to prove the rule, since the capacity to make scientific and mathematical statements accurately, precisely and impersonally reveals assimilation of the cultural ideal of objectivity and an ability to imagine oneself outside the sytem of which one is in fact a part.

If dreams are messages with meaning, formulated by an agent, much of what I have said about verbal utterances must apply to them as well. The imagery and metaphors used, the clarity or vagueness, the congruity or bizarreness, the economy or diffusiveness with which they are constructed, must all provide information about the dreamer's experience, personality and imaginative capacity which is, strictly speaking, additional to the specific interpretations that can be made of particular dreams. This is one of the reasons why Jung, Calvin Hall and others have recommended that dreams should be studied not singly but in series.

For instance, if, to cite examples of dreams quoted elsewhere in this book, someone uses imagery from heraldry in a dream about discouragement, or imagery of agricultural machinery in a dream about submission, or imagery derived from social snobbery in a dream about identity, these choices of imagery all provide information about the dreamer's biography, since, rather obviously, heraldic images, agricultural equipment and the nuances of aristocratic hierarchies do not form part of everyone's store of images; present or past experiences, interests and aspirations must be being revealed by the use of such images.

All this would be both pedantic and obvious if it were not for a very crucial difference between waking utterances and dreams. If we are talking to someone, we are awake and know who we are and to whom we are talking—and even when writing we have some conscious conception of our role as a writer and the readership we are writing for—and the additional information revealed by our style and mode of utterance will commonly already be familiar to our audience; or if it is not, it will form part of what we are prepared or willing to let it know about us. In other words, the self-revelations of waking utterances are, by and large, voluntary even if unwitting and unwilled. The only important exceptions to this generalization are the utterances of people who have something to conceal; spies, imposters and people who wish to conceal their social origins or specific disgraceful events in their lives. In such people the self-revelatory tendency of speech is confused by defensiveness, evasiveness and pretentiousness and more or less successfully counteracted by dissimulation, which may be either willed, as in the case of lying, or habitual, as in the case of phoneys.

If, on the other hand, we are telling someone else a dream we have had, things are quite different. Even though we know who we are while we are telling it, there is some sense in which we did not know who we were while we dreamt it, since our dream self is someone other, or more than, or less than our waking self. The dream may indeed feel so alien that we report it as though it had no connection with ourselves at all and could not possibly reveal anything about us. Whereas when talking ordinarily, we operate from a known self, when telling a dream we render our self problematic by the act of doing so. Furthermore, when we consider our motives for telling someone a dream we have had, it becomes apparent that we are concerned either to alter our conception of ourself or to alter our audiences's conception of ourself. Intimates who tell each other their dreams seek, I believe, to enhance their self-conceptions by making each other witnesses of aspects of themselves which have not become assimilated into their waking selves but which are, they hope, emergent. Patients who tell their analysts their dreams hope that their analyst will be able to discover in them what it is about themselves that they do not understand; a pre-condition of becoming an analytical patient is the conviction that there is something about oneself that one does not understand.

As a result, the telling of dreams and, perhaps even more, the listening to dreams is influenced by the fact that dreams can be used to discover information about the dreamer of which he himself, by reason of repression or alienation, is unaware. Psychoanalysts listen to their patients' dreams not only in the hope of being able to find the meaning of each, individual reported dream, but also in the hope of gathering more general information bearing on their patients' problems: information about specific traumatic experiences, details of which may obsessively and recurrently intrude into dreams; information about infantile fixation points, which may be revealed by the recurrent use of oral, anal or phallic body symbolism; and information about habitual defensive manœuvres, which may be conveyed by the way in which the patient constructs his dreams.

For instance, patients who habitually use the manœuvre known as 'isolation', by which important memories, thoughts and wishes are segregated from the continuity of their being, not uncommonly divide their dreams into two unequal parts, the smaller of which has no apparent connection with the larger and, in the telling of it, is conspicuously unemphasized. Or they tend to locate their dreams in distant parts of the world they have never visited. The intensely anti-American I mention elsewhere in this book, who used to dream architectural impossibilities and modelled his waking deportment on an almost extinct type of English gentlemen, used also to dream short, obscure dreams, which he thought hardly worth mentioning, about places on the Soviet side of the Iron Curtain. These dreams were never interpretable, in the sense of being translatable into specific statements or wishes, but it was possible to deduce from them that his contempt for contemporary American capitalist society, might, if anglophilia had not intervened, have driven him towards the Kremlin. But in sober, waking fact, he had never visited any communist country and was dismissive of all marxist ideas.

However, the point I wish to emphasize here is that scanning dreams for evidence about the dreamer's traumata, fixations and defences is, in principle, something different from interpreting particular dreams; even though, in practice, these two activities may be hard to distinguish, since earlier dreams remembered by both analyst and patient will provide part of the context within which any individual dream is interpreted and will contribute to the analyst's familiarity with his patient's imagination which entitles him to make interpretations of dreams.

An analogous issue arises in poetic criticism. It may, sometimes at least, be possible to understand a poem better if one has read some of the poet's other poems and to discern meanings in it which would otherwise elude one. It may also be possible to discover a poet's religious beliefs and social and political attitudes, and even to make biographical surmises, by reading his poems, but it is by no means clear whether one is entitled to include these deductions and surmises within an interpretation of any particular poem. Anyone reading Donne's poetry can discover that he was familiar with the geographical discoveries of his time, that he was at home in the medieval worldview and at the same time *au fait* with Copernican heliocentric astronomy. It is, indeed, impossible to understand some of Donne's conceits unless one appreciates these facts about him. But it is by no means clear whether one is entitled to say that tension between medieval and Copernican views of the universe forms part of the meaning of individual poems, even though it must have played an important part in his life. The difficulty lies in knowing how far one can go in assuming that the whole of a person is contained, expressed and distilled in each of his imaginative products. Does the part always include the whole, or is that a romantic, neo-platonist and psychoanalytical illusion? Psychoanalytical case-histories which are presented in the form of an extended dream interpretation raise the same problem: where does exegesis stop and reading more into a dream—or a poem—than is really there begin?

Dreams of Patients in Psychoanalysis

The dreams of patients in psychoanalytical treatment acquire a number of extrinsic meanings and meta-meanings additional to their primary meanings as messages from one part of the dreamer to another.

These arise from the fact that the patient-dreamer knows that his analyst wants to hear about his dreams, considers them to be suitable 'material' for interpretation, and may be predisposed to interpret them as communications to and about himself. As a result, remembering or forgetting dreams, telling or withholding them, telling them cursorily and reluctantly or enthusiastically and *in extenso* or *ad nauseam*, acquire meanings derived from the nature of the patient's feelings about his analyst and his expectations from him, these additional meanings being in principle and often in practice distinct from the meanings contained in the text of the dream.

Just as between hosts and guests the motives for offering food and gifts often have little or nothing to do with the actual nature of food and gifts and a lot to do with making or resisting overtures of friendship, so reporting or withholding dreams by a patient are often gestures designed to please, appease, annoy, overwhelm or impress the analyst, these motives being adventitious and additional to the meanings contained within the dreams themselves. Under such circumstances dreams—or more strictly the telling of them—themselves become symbols, any particular dream representing a gift given or withheld, a challenge to test the analyst's skill and pretensions, a red herring to divert his attention from the person of the patient by embroiling him in the subtleties, ingenuities and obscurities of his dreams.

Furthermore, since patients only enter analytical treatment

because they are in distress of some kind and form 'transferences' of greater or lesser intensity, the person of the analyst, his voice, his mannerisms, his utterances, the objects in his consulting room, all readily become part of his store of significant images. As a result, the dreams of patients in analytical treatment tend to contain allusions and references to the analyst and his ambience, and to include messages which are, in the first instance, to and about him—but only in the first instance and not finally, since transference determines that the analyst becomes a symbol in the patient's mind for significant figures in his present and past and for aspects of his own self. Insofar as the analyst sticks to his interpretative guns and only says things to his patient that the patient, were it not for resistance, could say of and to himself, the interpersonal dialogue between analyst and patient is an actualization of a potential intrapersonal dialogue within the patient's mind.

This inclusion or intrusion of images of the analyst into the dreams of his patients has a number of curious consequences.

First, it may seduce the analyst into supposing that his patients' dreams really are about himself and into assuming that dreams have an interpersonal not intrapersonal communicative function.

Secondly, the revival through transference of the patient's feelings about his past leads to reactivation or resurrection of imagery, particularly body imagery, relating to childhood and infancy—a process enhanced by the fact that the analyst's interpretations tend themselves to be couched in such imagery. As a result, the dreams of patients in analysis contain imagery derived from breast-feeding, urinating, defaecating, being bathed, sitting on laps, lying in the parents' bed, more frequently than do the dreams of persons not in analysis; this at least is the impression one gets from comparing dreams cited in the psychoanalytical literature with those collected by Calvin Hall[11] from persons not in treatment. The criteria for deciding when such childhood body imagery in dreams derives from the analyst's interpretative habits and when it is based on a true recapture of childhood bodily experience are theoretically most obscure, but in practice the essential criterion appears to be the presence or absence of a conviction, shared by both analyst and patient, that something from the past is being relived not just talked and speculated about.

Thirdly, the fact that dreams of patients in analysis frequently contain allusions to the analyst often makes it difficult to justify interpretations of them to third parties, since their essential metaphors may hinge on details of the analyst's person or consulting room (the shape of his nose, his accent, the colour of his couch, or carpet or the walls of his consulting room) which have during the course of the analysis been endowed with some idiosyncratic meaning by the patient which it would be difficult and tedious, and sometimes indeed embarrassing, to explain publicly. In this respect the telling and interpreting of dreams during analytical treatment resembles interchanges between intimates: their highly allusive quality makes them readily understood by the participants but difficult to explain to others.

Fourthly, in so far as the analyst fails to preserve his anonymity and the patient possesses an impression of his actual qualities and information about his personal life, his career, his writings, the dreams of the patient may include symbolic representations of comments and criticisms that he is in process of formulating about the analyst. For instance, patients who are training to become analysts themselves may hear their analyst speak at a scientific meeting and later have dreams in which they appear to be assessing his performance, dreams in which their horse is or is not winning the race, a boat is or is not sailing too close to the wind, a band wagon must or must not be jumped onto. Such dreams, and indeed all dreams that concern themselves with the actual nature of the analyst, are inspired not by idle curiosity but by something much more fateful: doubts as to whether it is safe to reveal oneself to someone before one knows whether he can accept criticism gracefully, doubts as to whether it is safe to criticize someone on whom one has become dependent and from whom one hopes to

61

receive cure and, in the case of trainee analysands, professional qualification.

Action Language

In a series of papers and books culminating in *A New Language for Psychoanalysis*,[12] the American psychoanalyst Roy Schafer has proposed that the findings of psychoanalysis should be reformulated in what he calls Action Language. Action Language assumes that psychoanalysis is not a natural science but one of the humanities; it dispenses with all concepts borrowed from physics, chemistry and biology and seeks instead to formulate all statements about human behaviour and feeling in terms of a person or agent who acts—not in response to causes which impel him but for reasons which seem to him to be cogent.

Some passages in this book can be read as attempts to apply action language to dreams and assume that, strictly speaking, there are no such phenomena as dreams, but rather persons who dream, who perform the action of constructing meaningful imaginative sequences; and that interpreting dreams is essentially a process of ascertaining the dreamer's reasons for confronting himself with these imaginative sequences; in other words elucidating what ideas, feelings and insights he is trying to express and communicate to himself—or, in the case of people who report their dreams to someone else, to that other person.

According to this view of dreaming, the general theory of dreams concerns itself with three questions.

First, what range of thoughts and feelings may be expressed or formulated in dreaming? Is it identical with, or more or less extensive, than, the range of thoughts and feelings with which we concern ourselves while awake? The answer to this first question seems to be that in one respect the range is more extensive and in another respect it is less extensive. On the one hand we seem to be less restricted by personal and social hypocrisies while asleep and dreaming than we are while awake, and may in fact dream of many things that while awake we would never, we like to think, even dream of doing. On the other hand we seem to be more egocentric while dreaming than we are while awake. It seems to be our own pleasure, happiness, suffering, pride, shame, survival and destiny, not that of others, with which we are concerned while asleep. Calvin Hall[13] reports that he was collecting dreams from American students during the last few days of the war with Japan and did not encounter a single reference to the dropping of the atomic bomb on Hiroshima. In this sense dreaming is an egotistic activity just as sleep itself is.

Secondly, what are the 'grammatical' rules—not scientific laws—governing the construction of those imaginative sequences we call dreams, and what relation have these rules to the true grammatical rules governing the formation of sentences formulated while awake? The answer to this second question seems to be that dreaming obeys the rules of non-discursive symbolism. Unlike discursive language in which permanent, conventionalized units of meaning are successively understood and gathered together to form an overall meaning, that of the sentence understood as a whole, dream 'language' consists of transient, private images which derive their meaning from their relations within the total structure that constitutes the dream. Or rather, since dreams differ from sentences in having no clearly defined beginning and end, and in being blurred at the edges as well, from their relations within the total structure from which the remembered, reported dream has emanated; this total structure being in principle the dreamer's whole mind or being.

Thirdly, why, if dreams are meaningful utterances couched in non-discursive symbolism, are they commonly not understood by the person who dreams them? If dreams are messages or letters to oneself, why does the dreamer so frequently construct the dream in such a way that he cannot elucidate it himself? There seem to be two current answers to this question.

The first is that the message is, as it were, deliberately constructed so as not to be understood and some of the rules governing the formation of dreams are devices to ensure that they will be undecipherable by the dreamer when he has awoken. This answer, which was Freud's, assumes that the messages in dreams concern matters about which the waking self does not want to know and implies the existence of conflict between two different selves, one of which seeks to express wishes, feelings and thoughts which the other does not want to hear about, the dream being a device by which the dreamer achieves a hypocritical compromise. One self is allowed its say provided the other self can assert that it is talking nonsense and need not listen to what it is saying, symbolism being the specific device by which this compromise is achieved. According to this view, dreams are essentially disguised expressions of wishes, thoughts, and feelings which, if expressed openly, would have awakened the sleeping dreamer, and which, if understood by him, would disturb his equanimity and compel him to alter his conception of himself, dreaming is strictly speaking not the creation of an agent who is trying to communicate something true but a defensive, hypocritical manœuvre engaged in by someone who is trying to deceive himself, and dream-interpretation is a technique for elucidating the truth that lies concealed in false messages.

The alternative view of dreaming is that visual, symbolic, non-discursive mental activity is just simply the way in which we think while asleep and that there is no reason to suppose that symbolism is essentially a device by which dreamers deceive and obfuscate themselves, even though it may on occasion be used as such. According to this view dreams are, or can be, true, straightforward messages from one aspect of oneself to another, and dream interpretation is a process of translation of one language into another, a process which requires knowledge of the grammatical rules governing both but does not necessarily involve overcoming the dreamer's waking self's reluctance to accept the truth of the message.

The evidence that this view of dreams, which was Jung's, is correct is of two kinds: first, that provided by people who, when they consult psychoanalysts, do not display the expected resistance to dream-interpretation, who are, as the jargon has it, in touch with their own unconscious; and secondly, the fact that the imagery accompanying orgastic dreams may, in one and the same person, at times be overtly sexual and at other times be symbolic, and it is difficult to imagine that one night a dreamer may wish to repudiate his sexual wishes and another night may admit them freely. In passing it may be noted that a passage in the 1914 edition of Freud's *Interpretation of Dreams*[14] reveals that Freud must have had patients who possessed a direct understanding of dream-symbolism and that he viewed them with deep suspicion:

> ... for a time there was an inclination to suspect every dreamer who had this grasp of symbols of being a victim of that disease (dementia praecox, i.e. schizophrenia). But such is not the case. It is a question of a personal gift or peculiarity which has no visible pathological significance.

The assumption that dreaming is the activity of an agent who sends messages, true or false, disguised or open, raises questions as to who this agent is and how many agents participate in the construction of dreams, which do not arise if one makes the conventional assumption that dreams are mental events or phenomena that one observes. If one asserts 'I dreamt' and means what one says, instead of reporting that 'I had a dream', is that 'I' the same person as the 'I' who remembers having dreamt? Freud, it seems to me, ducked this problem to the extent that he regarded dreams as phenomena which were subjectively experienced as external to the self, but resolved it to the extent that he postulated an impersonal agent, the Id or It, which expressed itself in dreams. His disguise theory of dreams seems to involve the assumption of at least two agents who participate in the construction of dreams, every dream being analogous to a communiqué issued by two antagonistic powers who have agreed to shelve their differences without admitting that they have done so. Jung, on the other hand, seems to have consistently rejected the idea that dreams are phenomena and to have regarded them as messages but to have had difficulties about naming the agent who creates them.

It would seem then that there are difficulties, some real, some verbal, in identifying or naming the agent who actively dreams. It is not the familiar, conscious, waking 'I', who is the recipient of dream messages, and yet it must, in the absence of any other candidates—apart perhaps from God—be part of oneself. And yet this part of oneself seems to lack some of the essential attributes of selfness—one cannot, for instance, imagine it willing—and there seems to be an inescapable need or tendency to think of it impersonally, as 'it' rather than 'I' or even another 'I', a tendency which is exemplified by the use by the Founding Fathers of psychoanalysis of such concepts as the Repressed, the Unconscious, the Id and the It. It would seem indeed that in attempting to pursue and locate the agent who constructs dreams we have entered territory where paradox reigns and language fails. The dream agent is some thing that is part of oneself but also more than oneself, that is personally impersonal and impersonally personal, that sends messages without ever willing or deciding to do so but only because it cannot not do so

The Self

Since we are unaware, while dreaming, that we are ourselves creating the dream that we are 'having', all psychologies that attribute meaning to dreams have to postulate the existence of two selves; one which is restricted to what we know of ourselves when awake and conscious and which is capable of acting, willing and reflecting upon its activities, and another which embraces the whole of the personality, including that part of ourselves that dreams. The former self is aware of its own identity and refers to itself as 'I' or 'me', the latter self, or Self, is experienced as impersonal and tends to be referred to as 'it' or 'one'.

The personal quality of the conscious self and the impersonal quality of the wider Self is reflected in the psychoanalytical division of the personality into an ego or I, which is largely conscious and can act, will, and, on occasion, become self-aware, and an Id or It which is largely unconscious and cannot act or will and manifests itself in dreams and imaginative activity. Poets have also described the impersonal quality of the source of their creative activity. For instance Rimbaud said both 'On me pense' and 'Je suis un autre.'

The relationship between these two selves differs from person to person. If the personal I self is sharply opposed to the impersonal It Self, the individual will possess what Jung called a Persona, a mask, a sharply defined and rigidly circumscribed personality, and his dreams will recurrently present to him figures, which Jung called Shadows, who engage in activities totally alien to his waking self and who attempt to break into his house. In the less personal language of Freudian psychoanalysis, such people suffer from character-neuroses, have rigid defensive egos and are out of touch with their unconscious. In Reichian terminology they are imprisoned in character-armour.[15] If the personal I self is habitually concerned to accommodate itself to the needs and expectations of others without taking cognisance of its own needs and nature, the individual will possess what Winnicott called a False Self, his True Self being submerged and, as it were, in abeyance—in Winnicott's view the False Self is also a Caretaker Self, maintaining the True Self inviolate until it is safe for it to emerge.[16]

If, on the other hand, the personal I self is on good terms with the impersonal It Self, the individual will be in touch with himself, not fighting himself, not hiding himself, not running away from himself, not searching for himself, and he will require neither persona, nor rigid defences, nor character armour. Such a person is healthy in the true sense of being whole, not divided.

Quite apart from the question as to whether health in this absolute sense does or could occur in an imperfect world, or whether it remains an ideal, the fact that growth and change continue throughout life makes it inconceivable that there should ever be a state of static fusion or identity of the two selves. Just as changes in the outside world ensure that there are always new experiences to assimilate, so changes within ourselves instigated by maturation and ageing ensure that there are always potential, emergent aspects of the Self which the personal I self has yet to assimilate.

Psychotherapies which use dream interpretation aim to diminish the division between the two selves by increasing the extent to which the personal I self recognizes that the impersonal It self is itself part of itself, i.e. that the two selves are ultimately one self. In Jungian terminology this process of fusion of the two selves is called individuation, but Freudian analysts have, until recently at least, preferred the more objective-sounding 'integration'. It is striking that Freud and Jung viewed individuation-integration in diametrically opposed ways. For Freud it consisted in the mastery of the impersonal Id by the ego, a process he once likened to land-reclamation; for Jung it consisted in 'the assimilation of the ego by a wider personality'.[17]

One of the obstacles to conceiving of dreams as having meaning and to recognizing that the images appearing in them are our own thoughts and not pseudo-perceptions is that, if they do have meaning, they must present the self to the self as its own object—an idea which seems puzzling and mysterious, since our usual tendency is to think of one's self as being the subject of consciousness, and whatever we are conscious of as being the object, and as being not-self just because it is the object not the subject of consciousness. Even when we look directly at a part of our own body or attempt to introspect some particular thought or feeling we have had, we seem to do so by dissociating that restricted aspect of our self from our self as subject and

68

regarding it as temporarily not-self. It becomes 'me' not 'I'. And to do anything else would seem as impossible as to see the back of one's head without using a mirror.

As Kant says somewhere, 'It is altogether beyond our powers to explain how it should be possible that "I", the thinking subject, can be the object of perception to myself, able to distinguish myself from myself.' Yet this is what we seem to be able to do while dreaming.

A rather pretty example of a dreamer identifying a figure and a thought in a dream as a part and thought of his own self is provided by a detail of Freud's dream about Irma (see Chapter 1, p. 29). Freud, Dr M, Otto and Leopold, the latter three all friends and colleagues of Freud, are examining Irma, a patient of Freud's, and Dr M has just pronounced that Irma's illness is an infection. The four doctors then momentarily fuse to become a single subject: 'We were directly aware, too, of the origin of the infection.' His speculations and imaginings about the cause of Irma's illness are at first distributed between the four doctors, but as soon as the diagnosis is made 'we' become 'directly aware' of its origin; and his thoughts cease to be imagined images and revert to being his own subjective consciousness.

According to Coleridge the function of imagination is precisely that of being able to convert the self into an object. 'The province (of the imagination) is to give consciousness to the subject by presenting to it its conceptions objectively.'[18]

CHAPTER 4

Metaphor and Symbol

Metaphor

Metaphor is the figure of speech by which one thing or process is described in terms belonging literally to some other thing or process; or by which the names and descriptive terms literally applicable to one thing or process are transferred to some other thing or process. Since the novel and unfamiliar can only be described in terms of the familiar, and the abstract can originally only be described in terms of the concrete, vocabulary is largely built on metaphor, and we use it whenever we speak or write, often without knowing that we are doing so. It must, for instance, be unusual for anyone using the word 'trivial' to be aware while doing so that he is describing a thought as though it were a road that had reached a trivium, a place where three ways meet and where presumably it is immaterial in which direction one proceeds.

The ability to use metaphor depends on the capacity to see a similarity between things or processes that are in other ways dissimilar; a capacity which seems to be intuitive, in the sense that one either sees the similarity or one doesn't. As Aristotle put it, 'a good metaphor implies an intuitive perception of the similarity in dissimilars'.[1]

Textbooks on grammar divide metaphors into dead and live; dead metaphors being those which have become built into language and do not usually evoke any image of the object or process to which they literally refer, and live metaphors being those which, as Fowler puts it, 'are offered and accepted with a consciousness of their nature as substitutes for their literal equivalents'[2] and do evoke imagery of the things and processes to which they literally refer. If I refer to an error as glaring, I am using a dead metaphor, since I do not expect my audience to conjure up an image of eyes glaring; but if I quote—it seems to be in the nature of things that one can no more create live metaphors to order than dream to order—Nashe and say 'Beauty is but a flower Which wrinkles will devour',[3] I am using live metaphor. That beauty is a flower may be dead metaphor, but that wrinkles may devour, not replace or obliterate, conjures up blight ('diseases in plants due to fungoid parasites'), worms, time, rodent ulcer (skin cancer induced by excessive exposure to sunlight) and is a live metaphor.

It is the contention of this book that dreaming is an imaginative activity and that the imagery occurring in dreams is to be understood metaphorically; and that dream interpretation consists in discovering to what subject or theme the concrete imagery of dreams metaphorically applies. Whereas, when used as a figure of speech, metaphor is used with consciousness of its nature as a substitute for direct statement, when used while dreaming, metaphor is presented as though it meant itself, and it requires the addition of waking, reflective consciousness to ascertain to what it applies. Or, alternatively, imagery in dreams fulfils a function the reverse of that fulfilled by metaphor in waking speech. Metaphor in waking speech adds to or defines more precisely and vividly a meaning already and consciously intended; imagery in dreaming lacks as yet the meaning that will turn it into metaphor. It is, as it were, a thought that has yet to acquire the author who will give it metaphorical meaning. Poetic imagery, which characteristically contains more meanings than the poet can have been fully conscious of when it first arose in him, occupies an intermediate position between the imagery of waking speech and dreaming. When Nashe wrote 'Beauty is but a flower' he probably knew exactly what he was saying, but the implications of 'Which wrinkles will devour' probably only struck him after the word devour had occurred to him as a rhyme for flower; in other words, metaphor in ordinary, prosaic speech follows meaning, metaphor in dream precedes meaning, and metaphor in poetry co-exists or oscillates with meaning.

As an example of the metaphorical nature of dreams, I cite a dream which depends largely on dead metaphor. A young woman dreamt that she was in a shop choosing shirts, taking several off the counter and draping them on the back of her current boy-friend. The shop apparently also sold fish which were swimming about in a tank—though, horror of horrors, one of her cats was drowning in this tank. This dream makes sense if one remembers that a dead metaphor allows one to speak of putting one's shirt on someone, another asserts that there are plenty of fish in the sea, and slang allows one to 'shop around' for a new lover. But, horror of horrors, if an ambitious woman does put her shirt on a particular man, does select one particular fish from all those available, something of herself may have to be submerged and perhaps die.

This dream also exemplifies another point about the use of metaphor in dreams. Since dreaming is a private, self-to-self communication, the rules of literary good taste are irrelevant and metaphors can be mixed, and clichés manhandled, in ways that would be unacceptable and absurd in speech. Although this young woman may well on occasion speak of putting her shirt on someone, or remind herself that there are plenty of fish in the sea, or decide that it is time she went shopping around again, it is unlikely that she would ever include all three metaphors in the same sentence.

For reasons given in the sections on Body Symbolism and Sexual Symbolism, the metaphors appearing in dreams tend both to be derived from bodily processes and to refer to them. Since, as I argue in these sections, we tend to be preoccupied while dreaming with our biological destiny, references and allusions to our own, our parents' and our children's physical behaviour and capacities couched in metaphorical terms occur frequently in our dreams. And since our imaginative apprehension of the external, not-self aspects of the world seems to be based on our capacity to perceive similarities between them and our own bodily organs, processes and sensations, it follows that external objects—other people, natural phenomena such as animals, plants and scenery, and artefacts such as buildings, tools, machinery and social institutions—appear in dreams as metaphors or symbols for our own bodily organs and processes and sensations. In other words, there is a two-way imaginative traffic between our own body and its activities on the one hand and objects in the external world on the other, so that each can supply metaphors to describe the other. As a result, if we are preoccupied with literal procreation and birth, we may dream of animals and plants, or of factories or publishing houses, while if we are preoccupied with writing a book, we may dream of conceptions—literal ones—pregnancies, and births.

Metaphor, both in waking and dreaming imaginative activity, depends on the existence of a store or network of images, at the core of which are those of our body, its activities and sensations, all of which can, unless impeded by inhibition, become metaphors one for another—in so far as similarities can be perceived in their dissimilarities.

Symbolism

Since the images appearing in dreams are virtual and do not correspond to objects that are actually being perceived, and since further they often make no sense if presumed to refer to the objects they themselves depict, they must often be symbols referring to or standing for something other than themselves. In other words, theories which assert that dreams have meaning and can be interpreted must of necessity also assert that the imagery of dreams is often symbolic and that individual images occurring in dreams may stand for objects and ideas other than themselves.

All this would be plain sailing if Freudian theory had not introduced a confusing complication by asserting that the symbols occurring in dreams differ radically from other symbols. According to Ernest Jones, whose paper 'The Theory of Symbolism' (1916)[4] remains the classic statement of the Freudian position, there is such a thing as 'true symbolism', which can be distinguished from what he calls 'symbolism in its widest sense' and manifests itself in, specifically, dreams and neurotic symptoms. In Jones's view words, emblems, tokens, badges and conventional gestures are not 'true symbols' and are only loosely and vaguely called symbols by those ignorant of psychoanalysis; true symbols, in the strict psychoanalytical sense, being those which represent ideas, feelings and wishes that have been repressed. 'Only what is repressed is symbolized; only what is repressed needs to be symbolized', the repressed ideas requiring symbolization being 'ideas of the self and the immediate blood relatives or of the phenomena of birth, love and death. In other words, they represent the most primitive ideas and interests imaginable.'

This classical psychoanalytical view of symbolism as something qualitatively different from the imagery and metaphor used in waking life derives from and is part and parcel of Freud's theory that dreaming is not simply the mind's activity while asleep but is a specific device by which repressed wishes can be granted hallucinatory fulfilment in disguised form without the dreamer becoming aware of the nature of the wish being fulfilled; so that, for instance, a dreamer can dream of mounting stairs without becoming aware that he wished to have sexual intercourse. According to this view, all dreams express repressed wishes and ideas, all interpretations of dreams are formulations of the repressed, primitive wish, and all images occurring in dreams are representations of one or other of 'the most primitive ideas and interests imaginable'.

Not surprisingly, many objections have been raised to Jones's attempt to distinguish sharply between true, psychoanalytical symbols and 'symbolism in its widest sense'. It offends against established usage, it creates well-nigh insuperable barriers between psychoanalysis and other humane disciplines, and, as the American analyst Kubie (1953) has said, 'There are no such discontinuities in nature as those who put the symbolism of dreams in a category of its own would seem to imply.'[5]

This last point is exemplified by the fact that it is not difficult to cite instances of people using imagery while awake and fully aware of what they are doing which would satisfy Jones's criteria for true symbolism if it occurred in a dream. When Balzac likened clumsy men making love to gorillas playing violins, or when Queen Elizabeth I said 'If I had been born crested not cloven, your Lordships would not treat me so', they must both have been fully aware of the implications of what they were saying and used images which do in fact frequently appear in dreams in contexts which permit their interpretation as sexual symbols. The same is true of the imagery encountered in dirty jokes, though in this case repression—or rather pleasure in overcoming repression—enters into people's motives for telling and listening to them.

Another objection to the idea that dream symbols always represent repressed ideas is the frequent occurrence in dreams of images which the dreamer appears to have derived from his stock of verbal metaphors: images of missing buses, of allowing grass to grow under one's feet, of beating about the bush. Sometimes, indeed, images may alter during a dream apparently under the influence of a more familiar or more suitable metaphor. A young woman dreamt that she was in a crowded bus with an unruly dog, which she put in her handbag and whirled round her head. At this point the dog turned into a cat, presumably under the influence of the phrase 'not enough room to swing a cat'.

It would seem, then, that the idea that the images occurring in dreams are phenomena *sui generis*, being 'true symbols' representing only primitive ideas and interests that have been repressed, should be abandoned and replaced by the idea that symbolization is a general capacity and propensity which creates metaphors when used consciously and dream-images when occuring while dreaming.

Finally, it must be remarked that there is something curious

75

about Jones's assertion that 'true symbols' represent 'the most primitive ideas and interests imaginable'. 'Ideas of the self and the immediate blood relatives or of the phenomena of birth, love and death' could as plausibly be designated 'fundamental' or 'basic'. The full implications, and the important grain of truth contained in them, of the idea that dreams are concerned with what has been repressed, and that what has been repressed are thoughts about birth, love and death, are discussed in the following section on Sexual or Freudian Symbolism.

Sexual or Freudian Symbolism

In view of the fact that it has become widely believed that Freud maintained that dreams are sexual, and that the images occurring in them are frequently if not usually symbols of sexual organs and activities, I begin this section by citing what Freud did in fact say on the matter.

The relevant quotations come from his Tenth Introductory Lecture (1916)[6]. 'The range of things which are given symbolic representation in dreams is not wide; the human body as a whole, parents, children, brothers and sisters, birth, death, nakedness—and something else besides.' This 'something else besides' turns out to be 'the field of sexual life—the genitals, sexual processes, sexual intercourse. The great majority of symbols in dreams are sexual symbols. And here a strange disproportion is revealed. The topics I have mentioned are few, but the symbols for them are extremely numerous.' Freud then goes on to list over thirty symbols for the male genitals and over twenty for the female.

Reading these quotations, and indeed the whole lecture from which they are taken, one is left with the overwhelming impression that in Freud's view dream symbolism is predominantly sexual. There are, however, two logical errors in his argument.

The first is a category error, that of comparing items that

are of different logical type and levels of abstraction. His statement 'And here a strange disproportion is revealed. The topics I have mentioned are few, but the symbols for them are extremely numerous', ignores the fact that the topics he designates 'few' and the symbols he designates 'numerous' are of different logical type and cannot, therefore, be compared numerically with one another. The topics -birth, death, the field of sexual life—are general categories arrived at by abstraction, but the symbols—umbrellas, revolvers, balloons, cupboards, apples, etc.—refer to specific objects. It is, therefore, hardly surprising that there are more symbols than topics symbolized, since the entities classified must of necessity be more numerous than the classes into which they are classified, and the 'strange disproportion' between topics and symbols, which Freud believed the study of dreams revealed, turns out to be no more strange than the fact that there are fewer genera of animals than there are species, and fewer species than there are actual animals—or that there are fewer parts of speech than there are words. The disproportion is, in fact, an artefact of thought, produced by the human capacity to classify experiences under general headings such as birth, death, sex.

Freud's second logical error consists in asserting, first, that 'the range of things which are given symbolic representation in dreams is not wide' when in fact the list of things which he says are symbolized in dreams—the body, parents, siblings, children, birth, death, nakedness, and sex—covers an extremely wide range of human experience, almost everything indeed apart from work, play and intellectual activity, and then, secondly, going on to treat 'the field of sexual life' as though it were 'something else besides' and in a different category to the other members of his list, when in fact it has intimate connections with them all. We only have a body because our parents once had sexual intercourse; we only have brothers and sisters because our parents had sexual intercourse more than once; we only have children because we have had sexual intercourse; birth and death are the first and last members of the series birth, copulation and death; and nakedness has obvious connections with birth, sex and parenthood. Here again Freud has committed a category error, that of detaching sex from the other members of his list and putting it into a class of its own.

If, however, one refuses to follow Freud in his categorization of sex as 'something else besides', it becomes possible to re-formulate his statement about the range of things that are given symbolic representation in dreams in more general, inclusive terms, without in any way reducing the force or bowdlerizing the significance of what he is saying. It becomes possible to say that the range of things symbolized in dreams embraces all aspects of man's life-cycle—and that the study of dreams reveals that human beings are more preoccupied with their biological destiny than most of them realize.[7]

Freud's idea that the great majority of symbols in dreams are sexual loses even more of its strangeness if one assumes that dreamers use sexual symbols not just to refer generally to sexual organs and processes but to formulate specific thoughts about them and that, therefore, the wide range of images that may be used to refer to sexual processes is a measure of the wide range of thoughts, reflections, puzzlements, expectations, disap-pointments, satisfactions and dissatisfactions about sexual matters that may be expressed in dreams. If a dreamer is trying to express something about the relationship between male potency and protectiveness, he or she might use an umbrella or an overcoat as a phallic symbol, but if he, or again she, wanted to say something about the ease with which male pride can be deflated a balloon might present itself as an apter symbol. Just as in speech, where the choice of the *mot juste* depends on the nuance of what the speaker intends, so in dreams the image chosen to represent a sexual, or indeed any other, idea depends on the precise nuance of what the dreamer is trying to express.

What is involved is not a thesaurus-like list of symbols which the dreamer has available for representing ideas of birth, love and death, but a capacity to detect and use similarities between objects and processes he has perceived in the outside world and his own body and its processes to construct metaphors with which to express thoughts about his biological destiny. And since the dreamer is communicating with himself and not with others, he does not have to confine himself to metaphors which would be comprehensible to others and are compatible with the social conventions, and he may therefore use metaphors which would be ludicrous, bizarre, incongruous or offensive if used in waking speech.

The construction of lists of sexual symbols is in any case a pointless and misleading activity; pointless, because such a list would in principle be infinitely long, there being no reason to suppose that there are any objects which could not be used by someone somewhere to construct a sexual metaphor; and misleading because objects whose images are used as sexual symbols do not in any real sense become sexual—any more than objects used to construct verbal metaphors become endowed with attributes of whatever they are used to describe. Roses remain roses, despite being perennially invoked as metaphors for girls and lips.

Body Symbolism

Sexual symbols can usefully be regarded as a sub-class of body symbols, that is images appearing in dreams which derive their meaning from the fact that the mind can perceive similarities between its own body and its actions on the one hand and objects and activities occurring in the outside world on the other. As Marion Milner[8] in particular has pointed out, there seems to be a general, innate tendency to apprehend all objects that are not one's self by likening them to organs and processes which are one's self, a tendency which enables us to assimilate the originally alien outside world into the inevitably and primordially familiar world of one's own body and its sensations,

79

and which provides us with a stock of images which we can liken to our bodies and its processes and to which our bodies can be likened. As a result, body images or symbols are available for making metaphorical statements about the outside world and for describing in concrete imagery mental processes; and images derived from the outside world are available for making metaphorical statements about our bodily and mental processes. Our mental processes would indeed be ineffable if we could not describe them in metaphors derived either from our bodies or the outside world.

The use of body metaphor or symbolism is not, of course, confined to dreams. Waking language allows us to endow countless objects with heads, necks, eyes, arms, hands, fingers, nails, trunks, waists, breasts, legs, feet and so on, and to conceive of winds whistling, cannons roaring, chasms yawning, rivers running, brooks babbling, etcetera. It is, in fact, full of metaphors which must have arisen and survived because of the ease with which the human mind can liken non-human objects to the human body. In dreams, however, the two facts that the dreamer is not confined by the proprieties and conventions of waking language and that he is likely to be preoccupied with what I have called earlier his biological destiny, facilitate and encourage the use of body symbolism in ways that would be disconcerting in waking language. I give three examples to make clear what I mean.

First, a patient in analysis dreamt that he gave his analyst a lift in his car, which turned immediately into a motor-cycle. A moment later he was carrying his analyst on his back and then, a moment after that, he was walking along with his analyst inside his testicles. It is evident that this man can conceive of a resemblance between a car, a motor-cycle, himself walking and his testicles, since he successively puts his analyst in or on all of them. And since he had entered analysis because he was sexually impotent, it is less than fanciful to assume that the resemblance between them consists in their power, borrowed in the case of the car, still borrowed but held between the legs in the case of the motor-cycle, actual but general in the case of himself walking, actual and specifically sexual in the case of his testicles. So in constructing this dream, he has used two images from the outside world, cars and motor-cycles, to symbolize the bodily power he knows he has and cannot use, and two images from his own body, himself walking and his testicles, to symbolize where this power should properly be located—and where, if he can take in from his analyst what he wants to get from him, it will be located. Those readers who have followed me so far will appreciate how difficult it would be to use the imagery this patient has selected to construct a discursive, verbal statement that did justice to the hopes and fears expressed in this dream.[9]

Secondly, a childless woman dreamt that her breasts were engorged with milk and her nipples covered with squid ink. Now since she was not lactating, never had lactated and, indeed, was never likely to, the image of her breasts engorged with milk must be a metaphor; she must be likening some, literally speaking, non-maternal aspect of herself to breasts engorged with milk, and the squid ink must refer to whatever it is that renders her breasts engorged, that is filling with milk that is not expressed, since squids secrete or, rather, excrete their ink in order to repel predators. She must, in fact, be posing herself a problem: why should someone who feels that she has a lot to give, whose breasts are engorged with what she should give, feel that she repels those who might wish to receive it from her? A not uncommon feminine predicament, which another woman expressed by using body symbolism the other way round; she dreamt that she prepared a salad for her guests and then grated her own skin over it. Here again it is difficult to imagine anyone awake and speaking using such imagery to express the dilemma of feeling simultaneously desirable and repulsive.

Thirdly, the same woman dreamt that she had to use a public telephone but the coins jammed and she had to loosen them. Somehow they became unjammed and copper coins poured out in enormous quantities all over the place. Here the body symbolism is not sexual or maternal but anal. The dreamer is likening a telephone box pouring out copper coins to a person (herself) being anally incontinent, and is expressing the fear that if she did become unjammed (disinhibited) faeces would pour all over the place. This fear itself derives from another aspect of body symbolism, the fact that various parts of the body, in this instance its openings, can be likened to one another, and fears originating in one can be transferred to another, so that, as in this woman, the need to love, which is naturally located in the genitals and the breasts, can be inhibited by an anal fear of being repellent.

These examples will, I hope, show how images of objects that are not self—cars, motor-cycles, squid ink, telephone boxes, coins—may be used in dreams to represent bodily processes, and how images of the body—testicles, the self walking, engorged breasts—may be used to express fateful thoughts about love and its impediments; and, furthermore, how dreamers use body metaphor and symbolism without reference to the restrictive conventions of waking language.

Birth Symbolism

According to Freud, and indeed Jung too, birth is one of 'the range of things which are given symbolic representation in dreams',[10] and emergence from water is commonly cited as a typical symbol of birth. This seems to be correct; dreams of someone emerging from a sea or lake or from a ship or a bus are common and often readily interpretable as being concerned with birth—the birth in question being either a literal one—the dreamer's own, his siblings', those of his actual or hoped-for children, etc—or a metaphorical one—the publication of the book he is writing, the film he has made, the re-birth he is hoping to achieve during treatment, etc.

Dreams in which a child is actually being born are not uncommon and, in women's dreams, both the baby and the mother may represent aspects of the dreamer's personality, the baby standing for either the new and better self she hopes will emerge or the worse self she fears will. Such dreams are common during psychotherapy, presumably because a psychotherapist's relation to his patient is many ways maieutic* and can readily be likened to that of a midwife to a mother in labour.

Birth, then, is one of the aspects of man's life-cycle which may be represented symbolically in dreams and also a bodily process which may itself be used to symbolize non-biological creative processes. Since symbolic descriptions of birth are common in myths and metaphors derived from birth are common in everyday language, it is to be doubted whether the symbolization of birth and the use of birth as a symbol in waking and dream life are all that different.

In view of the fact that it has been seriously suggested, notably by Otto Rank,[11] that birth is the traumatic experience responsible for neurosis and many other human ills—and that people sometimes claim to have remembered and relived their own births while on LSD trips—it is perhaps worth mentioning that dreams using birth symbolism seem never to include details which entitle their interpreter to make any inferences about whether the dreamer in fact had an easy or a difficult birth or was a vertex or breach presentation. This suggests that dreams about the dreamer's birth refer to his childhood conception of what it must have been like to have been born and not to any actual memory of the event.

Automobile Symbolism

Automobiles feature frequently in dreams, and their meaning is not exhausted by referring to the fact that they are powerful

* Maieutic. 'Pertaining to (intellectual) midwifery, i.e. to the Socratic process of helping a person to bring into full consciousness conceptions previously latent in his mind.' (*Shorter Oxford English Dictionary*.)

machines rather obviously capable of being used as phallic symbols. If an automobile appears in a dream, its meaning will depend on whether it belongs to the dreamer or his father or his mother or someone else, on whether the dreamer is driving it himself or is a passenger, on who is sitting beside or behind the dreamer, on whether it is closed, open or a convertible, a family or sports car, new, old, veteran or vintage, home-manufactured or foreign—and on what specific features of it are mentioned by the dreamer. Difficulties with the steering suggest anxiety about self-control, with the headlights or windscreen wipers suggest problems about insight and knowing where one is going; there is something flatal about the exhaust system; dreams of running out of petrol suggest fears about lacking energy or resources; dream of punctures suggest fears of being deflated.

I suspect that the relationship between a driver and his automobile has replaced the platonic image of the rider and his horse as the most apt and most used metaphor for expressing the great variety of relationships that can exist between a person and his passions. Modern man is more likely to dream of being at the wheel of his car, which he may or may not be able to control in traffic or on the open road, than of having the reins of his horse in his hands or of spurring it on to further achievements.

The fact that cars are designed to have more than one occupant makes automobile symbolism available for expressing ideas about the dreamer's relationship to those 'internalized' figures who may be experienced as disapproving or encouraging; they can be represented as back-seat drivers or helpful navigators.

Automobiles often appear in dreams as sources of borrowed or stolen energy. In other words, they often seem to represent the idea of a potency which has been acquired inauthentically, the dreamer arrogating to himself potency which in fact belongs to the car or its owner or its manufacturer, so that he appears to be being active and dynamic when in fact he is being passive.

A female analysand of mine once gave a pretty example of this. She dreamt that she was driving a green sports car at speed along a motorway, but as the dream proceeded the car gradually turned into the green couch on which she lay during analytical sessions. The confession implicit in this dream was that although she liked to believe that she was going places under her own steam, she sensed that her ability do so was in fact dependent on her passive relationship to her analyst. In this instance, the sports car *was* being used as a phallic symbol. The same patient once dreamt that a policeman stopped her while she was driving her car and asked to see her identity card, on which her name was given as 'hysteria'.

Animal Symbolism

According to Calvin Hall, who has collected thousands of dreams dreamt by hundreds of normal Americans, domesticated animals appear more frequently in dreams than wild animals do, and the three most dreamt about domestic animals are horses, dogs and cats, in that order. He also states that women dream of horses twice as often as men do. The horse is, he says, 'a pristine symbol of wild, lawless, licentious animal passion'; he nonetheless lists it as a domesticated animal. He also says that the horse usually signifies 'masculine sexuality since he is a large, powerful creature of great vitality and alarming impulsiveness'.[12] Power, vitality and impulsiveness must have been distributed differently between the sexes in classical times, since Artemidorus lists horses among his symbols for women. Regrettably, Hall fails to offer comparable interpretations for dogs and cats appearing in dreams.

According to Freud 'wild animals mean people in an excited sensual state, and, further, evil instincts or passions',[13] and small animals and vermin mean children and brothers and sisters.

If, however, one keeps it clearly in mind that neither

animals, nor any other category of things or creatures, actually appear in dreams but that, on the contrary, dreamers use images of objects with which to make metaphorical statements about themselves, it becomes obvious that listing standard meanings of objects 'appearing' in dreams is a pointless, methodologically unsound, activity. The question is not 'what do, say, animals mean when they appear in dreams?' but 'what imagery does any particular dreamer have available for constructing his dreams?' and 'what determines the aptness of imagery to express particular ideas in dreams?'

Using animals as an example: any particular dreamer has available for constructing metaphor imagery of all those particular animals he has known personally as pets, as farm animals, as sporting animals on which he has ridden or placed money, all wild or domesticated animals with which he is familiar, all animals he has read about and seen pictures of, all animals featured in legends and myths with which he is familiar, all animals featuring in the proverbs, catch-phrases and dead metaphors of the languages he uses. So if someone dreams of a lion, it may be the actual lion, of which as a zoo-keeper he has custody, it may be the image of lions he has acquired from books, films, visits to zoos or time spent in a part of the world where there really are lions, it may be an heraldic lion, or it may be the lion that features in clichés as proud and roaring but whose tail can be twisted.

The aptness of animals in general to provide metaphors must depend on the fact that in some ways they resemble human beings whereas in other respects they do not, the most obvious way in which they do being that they are born, live and eventually die, the most obvious way in which they do not being that they lack the power of symbolic thought. It must, indeed, be this fact that animals have drives, passions, motives, a will to live, but cannot speak about them or, so far as we can know, reflect upon them, that they have biological destinies but cannot conceive of biological destiny, which makes them such apt and such frequently used symbols for precisely those passions and drives which are hardest to put into words, both intrinsically and because they are liable to repression.

The aptness of particular animals to provide metaphorical imagery must depend both on attributes they really do possess —or which the dreamer believes them to possess—and on the qualities that have been attributed to them by myth and folk-lore and cliché. Elephants really are enormous but do they really never forget? Rats, like all rodents, really do gnaw but do they really desert sinking ships? Shrews must really be greedy since they have to consume their own body weight every day but are they really shrewish? Dogs really do follow scents and attach themselves to their owners but do they do either with dogged determination? And are female dogs really bitchy? Pelicans really do have remarkable beaks but they don't really feed their young with their own blood. However, when it comes to constructing metaphors, whether awake or dreaming, it is immaterial whether the animal, or any other object, alluded to really does possess the qualities or attributes attributed to it; it is enough that the attribution exists. As a result, dreamers, even contemporary dreamers, resemble the authors of medieval bestiaries who listed the actual, the mythological and the symbolic qualities of animals without distinguishing between them.

It would, however, be interesting to know why, if Calvin Hall is right, American women find horses such an apt symbol for masculine sexuality. Is it because American men do or do not resemble the American woman's conception of horses? Is the American woman's conception of horses based on her actual experience of grooming and riding them and, if so, does she find them easy to keep in rein, or has she ridden them in perpetual fear of them bolting? Or does she, perhaps, associate them with the cowboys who ride them in Westerns? And does she realize that most domesticated horses are either mares or geldings? One suspects that what Hall calls dream-content analysis, the inspection and enumeration of the imagery contained in the dreams of large samples of 'normal' people could provide illuminating material about the extent to which imagination concerns itself with actual experience or with the myths, preconceptions and communal fantasies current in different cultures. Do the English, and English women in particular, did Viennese women in Freud's day, also find the domesticated horse a peculiarly apt symbol for wild, lawless, licentious animal passion and masculine sexuality with its great vitality and alarming impulsiveness, or do they prefer some other animal or think of men rather differently? It would be intriguing to know.

Collectors of useless words will be interested to know that dreams which contain animals are theriomorphic.

Finally, a dream which is both theriomorphic and metamorphic. A young man dreamt that a bull charged down a village street, plunged into a pond, and turned into a swan which swam gracefully and serenely upon the water. This dream expresses, I think, the wish to acquire poise, to achieve ego-mastery of aggressive and libidinal impulses, to change from being a country bumpkin and a bull in a china shop into someone who is in the swim and in control of himself; and, more specifically sexually, that passion can be assuaged.

Clothes Symbolism

Dreams using imagery connected with clothes are common. The dreamer may be dressing, may be in a state of indecision as to which pair of stockings, which tie, which suit to put on; or he may be embarrassed to discover that he—or she—is inappropriately or immodestly dressed or is the only person to be undressed in a setting where everyone else is dressed—or vice versa.

The metaphorical possibilities of clothes derive from the ambiguous roles they play in personal and social relationships.

First, they cover nakedness but may by their line, cut or function draw attention to what they conceal. As a result, dreams about trousers, skirts, brassières, may represent thoughts about genitals and breasts and reflections about maleness, femaleness, motherliness, seductiveness, etc. Secondly, clothes transform their wearers from the body they nakedly and naively are into the persona they present to the world. As a result, dreams about putting on clothes may represent thoughts about the authenticity or otherwise of the front the dreamer presents to the world and the relationship between his private and public selves. Dreams of putting on clothes belonging to someone else or wearing a uniform to which one is not entitled suggest self-accusations of plagiarism and pretentiousness; including in the case of dreams of wearing clothes conventionally worn only by the other sex, sexual pretentiousness, i.e. laying claims to attributes believed to be the preserve of the other sex.

Thirdly, clothes can create illusory changes in the wearer's appearance, making him or her look taller or shorter, thinner or fatter, younger or older, cleaner or dirtier, than he or she really is. As a result, clothes imagery can be used in dreams to express self-accusations of hypocrisy, of deceiving others about one's age or youth, of passing oneself off as more or less desirable or available or vigorous than one really feels oneself to be, of presenting oneself to the world as a sheep when one really feels oneself to be a wolf, or as a wolf when one really feels a sheep.

Fourthly, clothes are status symbols and may denote the status one has, or lacks, or aspires or claims to have, by reason of one's income level, social class, age or sex. As a result, dreams in which the dreamer wears clothes which are in his own view inappropriate to his actual status, in which he presents himself as possessing more or less status and deserving of more or less deference than he in fact feels himself entitled to, may represent conflicts between feelings of superiority and inferiority.

Some examples: a professional woman arrived at work wearing only a dressing gown. She borrowed a blouse and a skirt from colleagues but refused the offer of underwear, protesting that her clients did not need to know anything of her private life. An advertising agent fell asleep at work after attending a business lunch and dreamt that his suit was covered with spots. A woman dreamt that she was at a cocktail party wearing a low-cut dress and her penises (sic) popped out.

Travel Symbolism

Dreams in which the dreamer is travelling towards some destination, encountering obstacles on his way, are common. They can usually be interpreted allegorically, the journey being the dreamer's life, the destination being either lover's meeting or death or arrival at whatever position in life signifies to the dreamer fulfilment, and the obstacles encountered representing the psychological and social obstacles with which the dreamer is contending. Anxious travel dreams often represent fears of missing opportunities, since buses, trains and planes may be missed and barriers may be closed just as the train or plane is leaving.

When the destination is named, it is more likely to derive its significance from its place in myth, folk-lore, and catch-phrases than from any actual role it may play in the dreamer's life. As a result, westward journeys are towards ageing and death, journeys to Rome hinge on the fact that all roads lead to it and refer to thoughts about love or death, journeys to Naples allude to the catchphrase 'see Naples and die'. Dreams of travelling by taxi or underground are not uncommonly dreamt by patients in analysis, the former because taxis charge by time spent on the journey as well as by the distance travelled and because, although the passenger decides the destination, it is the taxi-driver that drives, the latter because analysis is readily likened to a journey underground at the end of which the patient will, hopefully, surface and see daylight again.

The trunks, suitcases, bags and parcels carried by dream travellers represent either the impedimenta they carry with them through life—the burdens of guilt and responsibilities—or the assets and treasures without which arrival at their destination would be rendered nugatory and which must, therefore, be clung to at all costs. And since on the last journey we can't take anything with us, dreams about dying may concern themselves with holding onto or letting go of luggage.

House Symbolism

Houses in dreams seem to be used to represent the dreamer's body, his mind, his mother's body in which he once lived, and more rarely his father's family.

It is not difficult to see why houses can represent bodies. They have fronts and backs, front and back doors, and often front and back passages, eyes can readily be likened to windows, bay-windows and balconies may be curved like breasts—and food comes into them, is consumed inside them, and the waste products leave through pipes or have to be deposited in dustbins.

Their capacity to represent the mind seems to depend on their consisting of compartments—stories and rooms—with differing functions, which are at one and the same time connected and separated by stairs and doors. They are therefore apt images for the mind or personality conceived of as consisting of various functions or faculties, which should be connected to one another to form one integrated building, but which in fact all too often are not. Hence dreams in which doors are kept locked or previously unknown rooms are discovered or walls have been removed. Furthermore the contents of houses comprise relics of the biographies of the occupiers, and so the furnishings of a house may represent the dreamer's memories, the experience or learning with which he has furnished his mind, or the junk with which he has cluttered it.

An historic example of house imagery being used to represent the dreamer's mind is provided by the dream Jung had in 1909 which led him to formulate the concept of a collective unconscious. He was in a house which was unfamiliar but was nonetheless his house. After exploring two of its floors he discovered a heavy door which opened onto a staircase leading down to a cellar, a beautifully vaulted room, which looked exceedingly ancient—and beneath which another staircase led to a cave full of scattered bones and pottery, including two skulls. It was evident to Jung that the house represented his own psyche, that the ground floor stood for the 'first level of the unconscious' and the cellar and cave for 'the world of primitive man within myself'. Freud, with whom Jung was travelling at the time and to whom he told the dream, sought to interpret it quite otherwise in terms of concealed death-wishes towards, perhaps, his wife.[15]

Houses also vary as bodies and minds do. They can be tall and impressive or forbidding, they can be broad, squat, angular, curved, welcoming, shuttered, desolate, deserted, illuminated, sunny, dark; and some have fronts or facades which conceal less impressive interiors, while others are unpretentious. An American who hated all things American and always dressed like an old-fashioned English gentleman, complete with rolled umbrella, frequently dreamt of buildings which always had one thing in common: they were architectural impossibilities with, for instance, Palladian ground floors and Norman first floors. This man, one surmises, was haunted by the suspicion that he was a fake. Another man dreamt that almost the whole of his house would have to be pulled down, if ever electricity were to be installed.

It is, again, not difficult to see why houses can be used to represent the dreamer's mother's body. Their elemental function is to provide shelter and security and prototypically they are warmer, quieter, safer than out of doors; they enclose their residents who have to go out of them to go to work, to face life, and who return to them for rest and sleep. When houses represent the mother's body they are homely, comfortable and comforting, unless the dreamer is claustrophobic, in which case the house will be presented as imprisoning, suffocating and morgue-like.

The use of a house to represent the dreamer's father's family depends, of course, on the linguistic usage, which permits 'house' to mean 'family' or 'dynasty' and on the fact that in a vestigially patriarchal society like ours, surnames, houses, property and money are more commonly acquired from fathers than from mothers.

Food Symbolism

Since we would have no biological destinies if we starved and in health eating is a powerful appetite at all ages, images of food appear frequently in dreams just as they do in waking thought—and just as metaphors derived from food and eating occur frequently in language.

Sometimes these images do in fact refer to food, as may happen when people are hungry, but more often they are metaphors or symbols referring either to the sense of being protected, welcomed and cherished associated with being provided with food or with the sense of giving, welcoming, and nurturing associated with feeding others. Or they may refer, as in waking speech, to other appetites, notably the sexual, or to ritual, ceremonial and religious connotations of food.

It is, I think, probably true that people who are, in psycho-analytical terminology, 'oral characters' dream more frequently of food than do others. These seem to divide into two groups, those who wish to be fed and those who wish to feed others. Those whose abiding, predominant wish is to be fed are those who have sought to avoid the anxiety attendant on growing up into the world by hankering after infancy and early childhood when they really were, they fondly imagine, protected from all dangers by a loving mother who fed them. Such people display the same hankering in their waking life; they prefer soft foods to hard foods, sweet foods to sour foods, white meat to red meat, homely foods to outlandish ones, sweet wines to dry wines; they require frequent breaks in their work to restore themselves with sweets or confectionery—in England Mars Bars are a favourite

—or a nice cup of tea, and go to bed with hot Horlick's malted Milk to fend off night starvation.* Years ago I had a patient whose spirits always lifted when she saw an advertisement for Benger's Food, for she had been a Benger's Baby, a fact of which her mother, for some reason, was inordinately proud.

In children this use of food to provide consolation, comfort and reassurance that they still really are the centre of their mother's world passes unchallenged and images of food occur frequently in their dreams, but in adult life it forms part of an elaborate self-deception, with which others often collude, to pretend that life is entirely cosy and safe, that violence, passion, and uncertainty do not exist, that Big Mother is still watching protectively over them.

There may, I suppose, be people who succeed in living out their lives naively believing that they inhabit a secure world, well provided for, perhaps, by a very kind husband who rarely 'bothers' them or a maternal wife who shelters them from reality instead of helping them confront it, but when such people have the misfortune to enter psychotherapy, usually with the diagnosis 'oral dependent character with phobic tendencies' attached to them, a very different and disturbing picture emerges. They start telling dreams that are far from cosy, in which appetite is revealed as being not the gentle sucking of sweet, soft things but as predatory greed—often expressed in images of crocodiles and carnivorous beasts—in which strange foods may contain poison, and they may themselves like Little Red Riding Hood be at risk of being eaten. What has happened here is that therapy has conjured up the Shadow that lay dormant behind the Persona and has encouraged the dreaming self to assert that it has appetites more passionate than can be satisfied by sweets and nice cups of tea, and that it was not true that infancy and childhood were such a blissful time as the

* The until recently exclusively masculine obsession with drink, cigarettes and steaks is a more ingenious variation on the same theme, which depends upon conflation of symbols of security with those of virility.

persona pretends; that, on the contrary, mother was frightening and domineering and the child whined and snivelled. The patient I mentioned above who was comforted by reminders that she had been a Benger's Baby once dreamt that she and her mother were taking a house to pieces brick by brick—the dreamer knowing that whichever of the two was left holding the last brick would die. The message in this dream was that Life with Mother had not been an idyll but a struggle for power.*

The most obvious examples of dreams in which food represents ideas of giving and nurturing are those of cooking and serving food dreamt far more frequently by women than by men. Although these can, rather obviously, be interpreted generally as expressing ideas about mothering in both its biological and social aspects, the details of particular dreams may indicate that they are statements about conflicts and inhibitions in respect of achieving the right to be Mistress of their own House and Kitchen and all that house and kitchen may symbolize—and are, in effect, more concerned with power and status than with, say, wishes to have and suckle a child. A woman patient dreamt that she was cooking a meal and one of her guests took over the cooking from her, made a mess of it, and then laid the table all wrong. This is, of course, a dream of being taken over by others and feeling powerless to prevent it, despite knowing full well that the intervention will prove disastrous. It is relevant here that a surprisingly large number of mothers refuse to teach their daughters how to cook, being reluctant to share the power and status invested in cooking with them, and interfere in the kitchens of even their married daughters, who often feel unable to protest. The connections

* This struggle for power between mother and daughter seems to lie at the root of the now fashionable illness of anorexia nervosa, in which daughters may prefer to risk death by starvation than to absorb through food symbols of being possessed by mother. All the dreams quoted in this section were dreamt by women who, in their late teens or early twenties, lost for several months both their periods and all relish for food.

between preparing food and power are also shown by the fact that women notoriously dislike sharing a kitchen with another woman, and that offering to help a woman cook is not uncommonly interpreted, often correctly, as interference.

The fact that foods can be used to symbolize other appetites, notably the sexual, scarcely needs exemplifying since language is full of dead metaphors implying that all desirable objects are edible and taste pleasant, but in view of what I have said about the self-deceptive, defensive use of food symbolism it is perhaps worth pointing out that describing women as sweet, delicious, luscious, sounds saccharine to most modern ears. It is, however, perhaps of some interest that dreams containing images of food form only a very small proportion of those reported and interpreted by Freud.[16] This must mean either that such dreams failed to arouse his curiosity or that the ubiquitous presence of domestic servants in old Vienna cut his middle class patients off from the reservoir of imagery provided by cooking.

Freud[17] does, however, report several dreams about food (cherries, bars of chocolate, pears, and strawberries) dreamt by children, and he asserts categorically that 'fruit stands, not for children, but for the breasts' and, elsewhere, that fruit may also stand for what he coyly calls 'the larger hemispheres of the female body', by which he presumably meant buttocks.

Allusions to the ceremonial and religious connotations of food may also occur in dreams. A woman patient dreamt that on New Year's Day her male analyst, who was robed in purple, presented each of his 45 patients with a small loaf* marked with a cross, which his wife had baked for them, and a Prayer Book inscribed Trade Union. In this dream she envisaged a situation and a ceremony, which, if it really occurred, would solve all those problems of jealousy, greed and possessiveness which beset human beings and present themselves as 'transference phenomena' during treatment. If analysts' wives really

* I imagine she had in mind what I would have called a hot cross bun, but 'small loaf' was how she described it.

did bake loaves for their husbands' patients, they would cease to be rivals and become mothers to them; if analysts really could feed their patients as Jesus fed the Four Thousand, patients would have no reason to feel jealous of other patients or guilty about demanding too much of their analyst; if bread were really part of the Body of the Analyst he could be eaten without fear of depleting or injuring him. In other words appetites could be satisfied and possessiveness could be acted upon without ruth, without regard to the interests and frailties of others.

The '45' in the dream must, incidentally, be a pun on 'fortified', so that the analyst is represented as giving loaves to his fortified patients, and the Prayer Book inscribed Trade Union must be an allusion to both Comm-Union and to the fact that the relationship between a patient and an analyst is a trade union, in that the analyst earns his living by taking money from his patients, demanding fees from them in exchange for his interpretations. The dream is, in fact, part of a meditation on Give and Take, on how a union between two separate people can contain the demands each may make on the other and survive the greed of both.

In view of what I said in the section on the dreams of patients in analysis (see p. 60), it must be added that the purple robe was an allusion to a tie I do in fact sometimes wear, one which, according to another woman patient, is exactly the colour favoured by Roman matrons past their sexual prime.

CHAPTER 5

Various Types of Dreams

Traumatic Dreams

Traumatic dreams occur after traumatic experiences, i.e. after totally unexpected, shocking experiences, such as being involved in an earthquake, a train or plane crash, being bombed, mugged, raped, or being anaesthetized without warning or preparation—as occurs to children who are not forewarned by their parents or doctors as to what is going to be done to them. The essence of a traumatic experience is, in fact, that it is a sudden, unexpected, unenvisaged terrifying event in which the subject is a passive victim and in no way an active participating agent.

Traumatic dreams consist of more or less accurate repetitions of the preceding traumatic experience. They become less frequent and intense as time passes unless there are psychological or financial advantages attached to continuing to have them, or unless the traumatic event resembled some pre-existing fear of the victim, as might happen if someone with a neurotic fear of travelling really did get involved in a train or plane crash—in which case the traumatic event would be experienced as a nightmare come true.

Traumatic dreams differ from other dreams in not being susceptible to interpretation, since the traumatic events they repetitiously reproduce are invasions and intrusions upon the victim's psychological continuity and are in no sense creations of his own imagination or envisaged consequences of his own actions. They have, however, unlike most other dreams, an obvious cause, viz. the preceding traumatic event, and a common sense explanation, viz. that they are attempts, eventually successful, to assimilate an initially unassimilable experience, to convert an unimaginable event that has none-theless happened into a memory.[1]

Nightmares

Originally the word 'nightmare' referred specifically to a terrifying, paralysing dream of being oppressed and over-powered by a fiend (or 'mare'), monster, incubus or succubus— an incubus being an 'evil spirit or demon, supposed to descend upon persons in their sleep, and especially to seek carnal intercourse with women' and a succubus being 'a demon in female form supposed to have carnal intercourse with men in their sleep' (both definitions from the *Shorter Oxford English Dictionary*)—but nowadays it is used more loosely to refer to any frightening dream from which the sleeper has difficulty in arousing himself.

In view of the fact that nightmares still occupy a place in folk-lore and that many otherwise well-informed people believe that they are common, it must be stated that this seems not to be so. According to Hartmann[2] true, incubus nightmares have only very rarely been reported by subjects sleeping under laboratory conditions and very frightening dreams are 'not quite so rare', while Foulkes *et al.*[3] whom I shall have reason to quote again later, report that children chosen at random—i.e. without reference to their psychiatric state—talk as though they expect that the dreams they will have in the dream laboratory will be frightening ('scary') but that in fact they are not. Frightening dreams have, however, been frequently reported by addicts who have spent nights in dream laboratories during withdrawal from barbiturates, amphetamines, and alcohol.

Ernest Jones[4], in his classic *On The Nightmare*, which was written in 1909–10 but first published in English in 1931, is also of the opinion that nightmares are rarer than most writers on the subject have assumed, although he makes no attempt to estimate their frequency and defines them in such a way as to exclude many equally distressing dreams. According to Jones, true nightmares have three cardinal features: agonizing dread, a sense of oppression and weight upon the chest leading to difficulty in breathing, and a conviction of helpless paralysis. He states categorically that such dreams are 'morbid pheno-mena'* which never occur in healthy people and that they have a specific pathology, being 'an expression of a violent conflict between a certain unconscious sexual desire and intense fear',[6] the certain unconscious desire being, in both sexes, 'the feminine or masochistic component of the sexual instinct'; in other words, true or incubus nightmares only occur in men who are totally unaware of their passive homosexual inclinations and would be horrified to discover that they had any and in women who would be equally horrified to discover that they had heterosexual inclinations. Not surprisingly, Jones takes the view that nightmares are more severe, and possibly more frequent, in men than in women.

It is interesting to note that, although Jones refers to his own experience, he never once cites a dream of his own or one of his patients and that most of those dreams he does quote were dreamt in the eighteenth century or earlier. Although this may perhaps be due to his having been inhibited by problems of professional discretion, which in view of the date of writing and the homosexual implications of his thesis must have been more daunting than they are today, it also raises the question as to whether nightmares are culture-pattern dreams, about which I shall have more to say in Chapter 7; i.e. whether true

---

* 'My own experience has convinced me that in individuals healthy in a certain respect presently to be defined it is impossible by any physical or mental agent to evoke any state resembling that of nightmare, while in other individuals unhealthy in this respect nothing will prevent the recurrence from time to time of nightmare attacks, and further that these can be elicited in them by the most insignificant of morbid incidents'. Jones.[5]

nightmares were commoner in the past than they are now, and whether they occur in cultures—and today perhaps in sub-cultures—in which sons have powerful reasons for being submissive towards their fathers, daughters have powerful reasons for repudiating their sexual feelings, and the prevailing ideology makes it possible to attribute one's own sexual feelings to demons.

I must confess that I have myself never had a dream that would satisfy Jones's criteria for a true nightmare; nor can I remember ever being told a dream by anyone else that would do so without qualification.* I can, however, report a dream that was unequivocally terrifying and could, at a pinch, be interpreted along Jonesian lines, though it had, I suspect, more to do with power and autonomy than with sexuality.

Shortly after the last war, a young man sought treatment for the sole reason that several nights a week he was awakening terrified and drenched in sweat just as he was about to be dismembered by some complicated machinery into which he was falling. By a lucky chance his therapist was able to identify the machinery immediately as a composite of a threshing machine and an electricity generating plant, both of which had, it transpired, been familiar to the patient as a child on his father's farm. The nightmares ceased as soon as the patient recognized the source of their imagery, but it was only after several weeks of further treatment that he realized how narrowly he had escaped falling in with his father's, in fact entirely benign, machinations to establish him in a career for which he had neither inclination nor aptitude.

* It is, I suppose, possible that patients in analysis rarely have nightmares for the simple reason that they are in analysis and have, therefore, in imagination at least, a protector from ghoulies and ghosties and long-legged beasties and things that go bump in the night. Later in this section I quote two dreams dreamt by patients which sound terrifying but in fact were not. I have also been told dreams by patients in which evil figures have intruded upon the analytical session, emanating from either themselves or myself; such dreams have been disturbing, even distressing, but hardly terrifying.

This dream can be fitted into Jones's scheme by attributing symbolic sexual meaning to the threshing machine and generating plant and by saying that the dreamer would have been masochistic if he had submitted to his father's designs for (not upon) him and must have been tempted to do so if it required a terrifying warning from his unconscious to restore him to himself, but it is simpler to say that in his dream he was envisaging the prospect of ceasing to be a free agent and of living out his life not as his own man but as his father's creature. It should be added that his father came of a class and generation which took it for granted that fathers had both the right and the duty to order their children's lives for them, but also appreciated that in this respect times were changing.*

This dream or nightmare exemplifies a point which I suspect be true but would be hard put to prove. This is that in dreams in which the prevailing emotion is terror or fright—as opposed to anxiety, which I discuss in the next section—the dreamer is imagining some situation which threatens his identity, his very sense of being as an agent; that what is at issue is not what as an agent he shall do, but whether as an agent he will survive. If this is right, people who have nightmares in either the strict, incubus sense or in a wider sense are in big trouble; they are threatened either by external contingencies which they somewhere realize will prove disastrous or by stirrings of their own nature for which they are entirely unprepared. Jones quotes a nightmare dreamt in 1753 by a girl of fifteen the night before she had her first period. 'She thought some great heavy Man came to her bedside, and, without farther (sic) ceremony, stretched himself upon her,' Her father, who was sleeping in the next room, was awakened by her miserable groans, ran

---

* I should perhaps state explicitly here that Jones considered masochism to be a component of the sexual instinct and closely associated with femininity, where I consider it to be a form of submission, the adaptive defence which all animals use when confronted by a member of their own species more powerful than themselves.

into her chamber, shook her awake and was told the dream. One suspects that both daughter and father were in urgent need of an enlightening talk—from a woman. And more seriously, nightmares may be the first indication and warning of impending mental breakdown and, perhaps, of physical illness.*

Finally, it must be mentioned that dreams which in the telling sound terrifying may not have been experienced as such. A woman in analysis dreamt that she slipped while rock-climbing in the Lake District, hurtled down the side of the Fell, crashed through the roof of a house, and landed on a bed unhurt. If we really did, as Freud maintained in the passage I have used as this book's second epigraph, attribute objective reality to the contents of our dreams, all but the end of this dream would have been terrifying, but in fact it was not. All the dreamer was doing was thinking some such thought as 'After all my misguided strivings, after slipping up so badly, what a relief to be able to relax . . .' Another patient dreamt that a lorry crashed through the wall of her bedroom and pinned her against a wall. She woke up puzzling as to how and why it could have stopped, touching only her left thigh. This is the dream of an experienced analysand who is pleased rather than frightened that her defences are being broken down and that her elusiveness has met its match.

Anxious Dreams

Although classical incubus nightmares and even very frightening dreams seem to be rarer than is popularly supposed, dreams which are accompanied by anxiety are common and are probably within everyone's experience. In an earlier book, *Anxiety and Neurosis*[7], I argued that anxiety is not, properly

* See the section of dreams and physical illness later in this chapter for an example of a frightening dream occurring just before a physical illness was diagnosed.

speaking, a form of fear, as much contemporary psychiatric thinking assumes, but of vigilance; vigilance being that state of subliminal alertness with which we continuously scan our environment to ensure that we notice significant changes within it and can adapt to them by appropriate action. According to this view, fear is the emotion evoked by the appearance within our environment of something known to be threatening and dangerous, while anxiety is the emotion evoked by the appearance within it of something unfamiliar and strange, something which seems to demand a response but to which we do not yet know what the response should be.

One of the reasons why fear and anxiety are so easily confused is that treating a strange object as though it were *ipso facto* dangerous is a seemingly appropriate response to it. But although many animals and human beings habitually do flee from strange objects, others display curiosity, exploring it to discover whether it is in fact dangerous or whether, on the contrary, it can be eaten, played with or safely ignored. Domestic cats confronted with the noise of Hoovers or washing machines or with other pets, and small children meeting other children for the first time, display anxiety which may or may not turn into fear.

Anxiety, then, is a state of mind in which we are poised for action but do not yet know how we should act, and we all experience it when a danger, a problem, a test situation, or an opportunity, has been encountered but its precise nature is not yet known—when we do not yet know what questions we shall have to answer in an examination, what kind of audience we are going to face when we appear on stage or give a lecture, whom we are going to meet at a gathering of strangers, what diagnosis and prognosis we will receive when we (or someone close to us) fall ill, how we shall manage if separated from familiar, protecting figures and are compelled to fend for ourselves. This last instance of anxiety has been honoured with a special name 'separation anxiety', since it is, in a sense, the opposite of other forms of anxiety, being evoked by the prospect of the disappearance of familiar objects rather than by the appearance of unfamiliar ones, and plays an important role in the production of 'neurotic anxiety'; neurotic anxiety being anxiety provoked by objects and situations which seem to give no grounds for it.

Although this is not the place to discuss anxiety in any detail, it is perhaps relevant that it has close connections not only with fear but also with curiosity, intellectual activity, courage, hope and imagination. *Roget's Thesaurus* gives it as a synonym for both fear and desire and classifies it as a prospective affection, i.e. an emotion directed towards the future, and the future is in the nature of things unfamiliar and uncertain. According to Liddell,[8] 'anxiety accompanies intellectual activity as its shadow', the point of this aphorism being that intellectual activity seeks to master the unknown by understanding it but itself generates further uncertainty and anxiety by revealing unexpected pockets of uncertainty and ignorance in what was thought to be already understood. According to McDougall,[9] anxiety depends upon an assessment of the future and is the second member of the series; hope, anxiety, despondency, despair. A great-uncle of mine, a naval officer, used unwittingly to reveal the interconnections between fear, anxiety, courage and imagination by dismissing compliments to his courage with 'Nonsense, its just that I've no imagination.'

Anxiety, then, is not essentially a neurotic phenomenon, though it may on occasion be one, but an emotion which we all experience intermittently throughout life, since both our environments and our bodies, our psychesomas, change in ways which confront us recurrently with unfamiliar situations which demand actions, reactions and readjustments the nature of which we cannot immediately define. Furthermore, it is an emotion which we can and do engender within ourselves by imagining, envisaging and rehearsing situations which we will, may or might encounter in the future. So, since actual and imagined, prospective anxiety forms an unavoidable part of the human condition and plays a continuous or at least recurrent part in our waking life, it is hardly surprising that we at times dream anxiously; and the presence of anxiety in our dreams can be taken as evidence of the similarity between dreaming and waking imaginative activity: they both concern themselves with imagined and envisaged situations, and an element of uncertainty and unfamiliarity must, of necessity, enter into all situations which are not or have not yet become actual. It is my impression that people have more anxious dreams during adolescence, during midlife crises, and during the throes of personal and professional upheavals, than they do when their lives are on an even keel. Later in this book I shall cite experimental evidence suggesting that 'worried' people who 'feel their problems rather than push them aside' and people who are 'reprogramming' themselves both sleep and dream more than conventional 'pre-programmed' types.

Although this way of looking at anxious dreams seems to me to be correct so far as it goes, there are several further things to be said about anxiety occurring in dreams.

First, if the thesis being put forward in this book is right and dreams are messages from parts of the self of which the waking self is unaware, or from a more total self which the waking self cannot embrace, then many dreams will be accompanied by anxiety, since their message will concern aspects of human nature which the waking self has turned away from and has lost any sense of familiarity with. In such dreams the dreamer is confronted by a memory, a wish, a thought, a prospect, which seems alien and unfamiliar, but nonetheless seems to demand some response without it being clear what that response should be. Inwardly directed vigilance has encountered something which it cannot interpret and to which it does not know how to react.

When these unfamiliar, disowned aspects of the self have become organized into what Jung called a 'shadow', i.e. another alien self very unlike the mask or persona the individual habitually wears, anxious dreams of being intruded upon by a stranger will occur. I have already given an example of such a dream in Chapter 2 where I cited a meticulous bank official who dreamt recurrently that a stranger was trying to break into his house. When, on the other hand, these unfamiliar aspects of the self remain discrete wishes, emotions or memories, we get a kind of dream which Freud must have had in mind when he formulated his wish-fulfilment theory of dreams. If the wish is sufficiently disguised, it will not be recognized as one, will pass the censor, and will not arouse anxiety. If, on the other hand, it is recognized as a wish but not as one of the self's own wishes, it will arouse anxiety. To be confronted by a wish—or an emotion or indeed a thought of any kind—which one cannot identify as one of one's own, and which would compel one to redefine one's conception of oneself if one did, is disconcerting, to say the least. As Freud said à propos of anxiety dreams, 'Thus a dreamer in relation to his dream wishes can only be compared to an amalgamation of two separate people who are linked by some strong element in common';[10] and one may voice wishes, or remember events, or express emotions, which the other repudiates.

Secondly, Freud was well aware that anxiety dreams are, on the face of it, powerful objections to his wish-fulfilment theory of dreams. He used three different arguments to persuade himself and his readers that nonetheless they do not constitute exceptions to it. First, he maintained that anxiety in dreams was the result of a failure in repression, of 'a breach in the compromise' normally arrived at between unconscious wishes and the dreamer's ego.[11] Secondly, he asserted, rather than argued, that translation of the manifest content of an anxiety dream into its latent content regularly does reveal the presence of an unconscious wish and that people who raise anxiety dreams as an objection to his theory have failed to appreciate the distinction between manifest and latent content. This is the line he takes in the *Introductory Lectures*. And thirdly, he insisted that anxiety in dreams forms part of the psychology of the neuroses not of dreams. 'The theory of anxiety-dreams, as I have repeatedly declared, forms part of the psychology of the neuroses.' 'Anxiety in dreams, I should like to insist, is an anxiety problem, not a dream problem.'[12]

This last argument turns out to be of greater importance than Freud's own texts on dreams reveal. At the time that he formulated his wish-fulfilment theory of dreams, Freud believed that anxiety is a form or transformation of libido. So he must have held that the occurrence of anxiety during a dream was itself evidence that its latent content included a sexual wish and that the common apparent objections to his theory were in fact evidence in favour of it. But one has to look elsewhere than in his discussions of anxiety dreams to discover this.

For instance, to his paper on Little Hans (1909).[13] When Little Hans at the age of $4\frac{3}{4}$ told his mother 'When I was asleep I thought you were gone and I had no Mummy to coax [i.e. caress, cuddle] with', Freud calls this an anxiety dream and interprets the anxiety ('I thought you were gone') not as separation anxiety but as transformed libido and as evidence for the presence of sexual longings in the latent content of the dream. As a result he does not consider the possibility that Little Hans was confronting himself with an important fact of his biological destiny, viz. that one day, of necessity, his mother would be gone and he would have no Mummy to cuddle with.

However, the interesting point here is that in the 1920s Freud[14] abandoned his own idea that anxiety is transformed libido and replaced it by a theory of anxiety very similar to the one I have adopted here—that anxiety is a danger-signal aroused by unacceptable impulses and initiating defences— without, however, altering his theory of dreams to take account of the fact that he had himself removed one of its foundations.

In other sections of this book, I have cited dreams accompanied by anxiety; examination dreams, dreams of being inappropriately dressed or undressed, of wild animals prowling outside a stockade, of missing trains, of discovering unexplored parts of one's house, and all the examples of waking anxiety I gave early in this section are situations of which people not uncommonly dream. It is therefore unnecessary for me to give further examples here. What I have been suggesting in this section is that such dreams either confront the dreamer with thoughts, memories and wishes which he has disowned and does not recognize as his own, or remind him of the relevance to his present uncertainties of past occasions on which he was uncertain and anxious (e.g. examination dreams), or envisage the prospect of losing present sources of security and satisfaction (e.g. Little Hans's dream of his mother having gone and all dreams in which loved people, things, places or ideals are being threatened, whether by fate or by one's own ambivalence).

I must, however, cite a dream which shows that it is possible to dream about anxiety—which is not the same thing as having a dream which arouses anxiety. A man dreamt that he was living in a coastal town when it received news that a tidal wave was approaching. The mayor of the town ordered alarm bells to be sounded to enable the inhabitants to take unspecified precautions. The dreamer then woke up. Here the dreamer reacts with the idea of anxiety, of heightened vigilance, long before the tidal wave materializes, and wakes up before he is anywhere near confronting himself with whatever aspect of himself the tidal wave symbolizes. Waking up before anxiety has been aroused, or before it has become distressing, or before the meaning of the dream has declared itself, is analogous to fleeing from an unfamiliar situation instead of exploring it— and to breaking off a conversation to prevent the other person telling one unwelcome home truths.

Oedipal Dreams

According to Calvin Hall,[15] the *dramatis personae* of 85% of dreams consists of three persons, the dreamer and one man and one woman, and the theme of such threesome dreams is usually jealousy. The other man or woman is not infrequently the dreamer's father or mother and is frequently an older man or woman. His collection of dreams includes several in which incest occurs, and many more in which the dreamer himself notices the resemblance of the desired figure to his own parent or in which the figures of parents and spouses, lovers, or fiancé(e)s are condensed.

Not surprisingly, Calvin Hall claims that by studying the dreams of normal people he has verified what Freud discovered during the treatment of emotionally disturbed patients.

The frequent occurrence of oedipal dreams supports not only Freud's formulations about the oedipus complex but also the wider idea, propounded elsewhere in this book, that throughout life we are preoccupied with our biological destiny and that our parents' relationships with one another, with ourselves and their other descendants, constitute an important part of that destiny.

Convenience Dreams

These are dreams in which the dreamer imagines that he is actually doing what he will in fact shortly have to wake up to do; in which, for instance, he dreams that he gets out of bed to pass water when he has in fact got a full bladder. Such dreams fit very nicely into Freud's hallucinatory wish-fulfilment theory of dreams, since they represent as enacted a wish of the dreamer and, if full bladders could be emptied by dreaming of doing so, they would enable the dreamer to go on sleeping.

Sexual dreams accompanied by orgasm are sometimes regarded as convenience dreams, the underlying assumption being that the need for orgasm is determined, rather simply, by tension within the genital organs that demands discharge.

These are discussed in the next section. Dreams in which the dreamer wakes up, dresses, goes to work, etcetera, can also be regarded as convenience dreams, but they may raise questions about the dreamer's reasons for wishing to remain asleep rather than wake up—questions about the value the person puts on sleep and the reasons for his disinclination to resume waking life again.

Orgastic Dreams

Almost all men have had dreams which culminate in orgasm and ejaculation, and in adolescence they are common. The imagery of such dreams is either overtly sexual or symbolic, and the same dreamer may use either type of imagery, a fact which is a powerful argument against the Freudian assumption that the function of symbolization in dreams is to disguise the nature of the wish expressed in the dream.

According to Kinsey, the sexual dreams of inexperienced women are essentially 'romantic', but 'occasional dreams to the point of orgasm occur in a considerable proportion of mature females'.[16]

The implication of such observations is that orgastic dreams are simply the result of sexual tension demanding relief, and that women are more dependent on sexual experience than men for discovering how to relieve tension by autistic hallucination during sleep. I find myself sceptical of both propositions, and the following quotation from Oswald shows that the tension is not where it is popularly supposed to be located.

Men whose spinal cords have been shattered through injury, so that there is no longer any nervous connection between their brains and their lower bodies, still have sexual dreams in which they experience all the feelings and sensations of orgasm. The basis of this experience is not in their isolated lower bodies. It is wholly within their brains.'

Ejaculations and orgasms can occur during sleep without any accompanying remembered dream or accompanied by the conviction that there was no accompanying dream; the emotion and feeling tone during orgastic dreams is not always erotic but may be angry or anxious, and the imagery, whether overtly sexual or symbolic, often does not represent a sexual act, as it would if orgastic dreams were simple hallucinatory wish-fulfilments. It would seem, therefore, that dreams accompanying orgasm may represent not so much fulfilment of the sexual wish as thoughts about sex and its role in the dreamer's life instigated by the impending orgasm.

Calvin Hall makes much the same point when, after quoting a number of overtly sexual dreams culminating in orgasm, including one in which a young man dreamt he was having sexual relations with a detached female organ as though to say 'this is the only part of a woman which interests me', he goes on to say 'Sex dreams are rarely so simple and unadorned. Usually the sex impulse is framed in a larger, more complicated picture, the analysis of which yields considerable knowledge about the dreamer's total conception of sexuality and all its ramifications in his personality.'[17]

In Victorian times, when masturbation was considered wicked and a cause of both physical illness and insanity, orgastic dreams must have been commoner than they are today and have been a source of distress to those who had them, as the following quotation suggests. It comes from a pamphlet entitled *The Modus Propagandi of the Human Species* by John O'Reilly, M.D., a Fellow of both the Royal College of Surgeons in Ireland and the New York Academy of Medicine, and published in New York in 1861.

It sometimes happens that ripe bachelors and men of strictly moral habits, who lead lives of celibacy, but who indulge in luxurious or idle habits, as well as gratify their appetites with a considerable amount of animal food, and, besides, drink ale, porter, wine, or punch, to make them happy and jovial before going to bed, have the mortification as well as discomfort, on awaking from a dream, to find themselves surrounded by damp linen, in consequence of profuse seminal emissions. Here it is to be remembered, that Sir Astley Cooper says, a man in his health will have a seminal emission every ninth day, and that the mode of living above described promotes such an occurrence: although persons can command their passions while awake, they cannot control the operations of the mind when in a dream; the animal propensities will conquer the moral under such circumstances. Si expellas naturam furca, recurrit atque recurrit. [18]

Ernest Jones, in his book *On The Nightmare*, which he wrote just as the Victorian era was beginning to wane, took the view that the prevailing medical idea that orgastic dreams are due to physical tension in the sexual organs is in its way as superstitious and irrational as the preceding medieval idea that they were due to the activities of succubi and incubi; holding that both explanations have in common the wish to deny individual moral responsibility for nocturnal erotic wishes—they must be due either to demons for whose activities one could not be held responsible or to bodily processes over which one has no control and which bear no relation to one's wishes.

. . . all erotic wishes without exception that disturb sleep have to overcome a certain amount of internal opposition, some being, of course, more heavily censured than others. Even at the present day it is customary for nocturnal emissions to be ascribed rather to some 'natural' physical activity on the part of the sexual apparatus rather than to any actual wishes that set this apparatus in operation. The tendency has thus always been to avoid any personal responsibility for nocturnal erotic wishes, even those most lightly censured, and to ascribe them to some other agency.[19]

In Jones's view, too, simple erotic dreams, anxious dreams accompanied by seminal emission, and nightmares form a continuous series, the differences between them being determined by the nature of the sexual wish being expressed in them and by the degree of repressive repudiation encountered by that wish—so that an 'ego-syntonic' sexual wish, i.e. one that is compatible with the dreamer's moral standards, will lead to a simple erotic dream, while one that is totally abhorrent will lead to a nightmare—abhorrent wishes being incestuous and, in men, passive homosexual.

Finally, it should be noted that there is something paradoxical about orgastic dreams, since, if viewed naively, they are simply explained as expressions of sexual desire and discharges of sexual tension, but, if viewed more sceptically, they raise awkward and insoluble questions. Can it really be true, as Kinsey's observations suggest, that the sexual impulse demands discharge more peremptorily in men than in women, and, if so, is this a biological or a social phenomenon? Does nocturnal sexual desire originate in the sexual apparatus, as Victorian physicians seemed to have believed and popular mythology still does, or in the brain, as my quotation from Oswald suggests, or somewhere in the psyche whence wishes can set the sexual apparatus in operation, as Jones seems to have thought?

> Tell me where is fancy bred,
> Or in the heart or in the head?
> How begot, how nourished?
> Reply, reply.

Dreams about Menstruation

Not surprisingly, women dream about menstruation more often than men do. And for obvious reasons dreams about menstruation often voice hopes and fears about pregnancy, fertility, sterility and ageing and, in both sexes, ideas about the repulsiveness, unattractiveness and dangerousness of female bodies; the flow of blood being interpretable as either a sign of life and continued fertility or as an indication of injury. Women who resent the fact that they menstruate and men don't may have dreams in which they compel men to look at or handle soiled sanitary towels and tampons.

Dreams about menstruation may also express more general

ideas about creativeness. A woman dreamt that she was removing a tampon in order to allow her menstrual blood to flow; two days later she found herself writing poetry. Another woman dreamt that the institution she worked for had become too constricted to accommodate her menstrual flow.

The slightly disconcerting effect created by this last dream arises, I think, not from the taboo area from which the dreamer has drawn her imagery, but from the fact that she has perpetrated a mixed metaphor. She has tried to express her feeling that her creative energies lack sufficient outlet by comparing it simultaneously with the sense of frustration induced by working in a constraining institution and the pelvic sensations induced by an increase in menstrual flow. One of her earliest memories was of falling off her fairy-cycle, cutting her knee, and hoping that her father, who was medical superintendent of a hospital, would be jolted out of his usual remoteness by the sight of his daughter bleeding. So 'institution' also meant 'father' and 'menstrual flow' her filial love to which he did not respond.

Children's Dreams

There seem to be wide and irreconcilable discrepancies of opinion about children's dreams. On the one hand, Calvin Hall, who collects dreams of persons not in therapy, thinks that 'what little knowledge we have of children's dreams suggests that their dreams are much more complex and much more dreadful than has previously been thought';[20] and Neubauer,[21] who is a child psychiatrist and analyst, says that children of 2 tend to dream of being bitten or chased, that children of 4 tend to dream of animals and of good and bad people, who either protect or attack them, and that children of 5 or 6 dream of being killed or injured and of seeing ghosts. On the other hand, Freud and Ernest Jones both thought that children's dreams are simple, 'sensible and intelligible', 'logical and co-

ordinate', and 'easy to recognize (as) ... the imaginary fulfilment of an ungratified wish';[22] and Foulkes et al.,[23] who
collected children's dreams under laboratory conditions, state
'first, that dreams of the child are generally realistically
related to his waking life, and second, that they become
relatively more bizarre and unpleasant for children with
some dysfunction in waking personality.' They also, as already
mentioned earlier, report that their subjects talked as though
they expected their dreams to be 'scary' but that the dreams
they actually reported in the laboratory were not.

These striking differences of opinion become a little less
surprising if one appreciates that Freud and Jones were
committed to the theoretical belief that dreams are hallucinatory wish-fulfilments and that it suited their book to believe
that children at least demonstrate this fact without the com-
plications introduced by the distorting effect of symbolism;
that Neubauer's generalizations are based on the dreams of
children whose parents were sufficiently worried about them
to bring them for psychiatric treatment; and that Foulkes et
al.'s subjects were not attending a child guidance clinic. Calvin
Hall's gloomy view of children's dreams remains, however,
entirely mysterious.

Children's reports of their dreams should, I think, be treated
for a variety of reasons with some circumspection. First,
children are still engaged in learning how to categorize their
experiences and in discovering what the words they hear adults
using really mean. In other words they are still exploring the
imaginative network constituted by language and learning
which words evoke what images and emotions in the adult
world they are growing up into and which connections that
seem obvious to them they must learn to ignore. As a result
their use of the words 'dream' and 'nightmare' will be affected
by their need to discover what these two words mean, what
distinction adults have in mind when they choose to use one
and not the other, and why adults react to one with curiosity
or incuriosity and to the other with, perhaps, concern. And

when they use a word such as 'goblin', which they are bound to encounter some time in a story read aloud to them, they will be discovering and confirming that it evokes in adults images of elves and sprites, whatever they may be, and not its obvious resemblance to gobbling.

Secondly, when talking to grown-ups, children are not talking to equals, but to people on whom they are dependent and who are more powerful than themselves. As a result, children may tell grown-ups what they think they want to hear, what they think will impress them or what they think will worry them. For instance, if a child announces that it has been having nightmares, this may not mean that it has just started having distressing dreams but that it has just encountered the word and appreciated that it is a more dramatic word than 'dream' and is more likely to create alarm and despondency in its parents. Or it may be behaving like those pretentious adults who insist on calling their headaches migraines, thereby insinuating that their headaches cause them more suffering and are deserving of more sympathy than those of lesser mortals.

Thirdly, having a 'bad' dream may in some families become a legitimized reason for a child calling its mother at night or for getting into bed with its parents, justifying nocturnal visits which, although frowned upon by those experts who create public opinion, the parents as well as the child may enjoy.

Fourthly, in a culture like ours which does not take dreams or the imagination seriously or, if it does, does so self-consciously, the motives for any adult, other than the mother, listening to a child's dreams are complex, to say the least, and children must, it seems to me, feel that something peculiar and bewildering is going on, if they are asked to tell their dreams to a child psychiatrist at a clinic, to a psychologist in a dream laboratory, or to an aunt who is a psychoanalyst. In the family described by Ann Faraday[24] in her book *Dream Power*, in which the children routinely tell their dreams to their mother, who interprets them, the children must, I believe, realize that they are competing for their mother's attention with her patients who also tell her dreams and have them discussed in her books.

Although these four considerations lead me to think that children's accounts of their dreams, and experts' accounts of children's dreams, should be viewed with some circumspection, I have no wish to take up an entirely nihilistic or sceptical attitude towards children's dreams. From a practical point of view, I think that Foulkes et al. must be right in their assertion that children's dreams are 'realistically related' to their waking life and only become bizarre and unpleasant in so far as their waking life does, while from a theoretical point of view I do not see that the view of dreaming being developed in this book requires any modification to accommodate children's dreams—with the single caveat that of the dreams of children who cannot yet talk, one can, of necessity, say nothing. Which is a pity, since it means that the first glimmerings of imaginative activity must always be a closed book—or a field for speculation and inferences that cannot be confirmed.

In view of what I have written earlier in this chapter about nightmares and anxious dreams, it will be apparent that I think that all children must have anxious dreams, since it is in the nature of things that they will at times be anxious, but that nightmares, in the sense of truly terrifying dreams, will only occur if something is seriously amiss, and it only remains for me to add here that children are more likely to have both than are adults.

They are more likely to have anxious dreams than adults are because more of the world is in fact unfamiliar to them, because they have yet to discover whether or not they could survive and cope if separated from their parents and familiar surroundings, because they may be expected to endure separations before they are mature enough to do so, because they lack—unless they are very fortunate in their parents—the imaginative equipment to assimilate their own intimations of mortality, transcience and the sadness of things (lacrimae rerum), and because they are growing so fast that their own bodily and emotional experiences may strike them with an almost traumatic impact. This last is, I think, most likely to happen to children whose parents have forgotten what it was like themselves to be children, treat them as though they were a different order of being, and lack the ability to respond intuitively to their changing needs, moods and capacities. To children of such parents, growth is itself an isolating, alienating experience, productive of anxiety.

Children are more likely to have nightmares than adults are because their autonomy as agents is in fact at greater risk. Whereas grown-ups can, although often at great cost, leave home, divorce spouses, ditch lovers, change their occupations, emigrate, even perhaps procure psychiatric treatment for themselves, if they feel trapped and in danger of losing all sense of themselves as an agent, children can do none of these things; there is no way in which children can divorce their parents, it is easier for a parent to abandon a child than for a child to run away from home, and although parents can take their difficult child to a Child Guidance Clinic, there are no Adult Guidance Clinics for children to take their difficult parents to. Children are, therefore,—and it is hard to see how it could be otherwise—at the mercy of their parents and, as self-awareness begins to dawn, they must realize that this is so. As a result children who have parents who believe that it is their religious duty to break their children's spirit or for their own reasons in fact set out to do so, or who threaten to abandon their children, to call in the Police, who beat or batter their children, or make impossible demands upon them, have good reason to feel that their identity and autonomy is at risk and are, I believe, more likely to have nightmares than are either adults or the children of less rigid, less authoritarian, more intuitive, more responsive parents.

Having painted this rather gruesome picture of the disparity in power that exists between parents and their children and of the effects that this may have, I must hasten to add that conflicts of will between children and parents, which may be sufficient to induce nightmares in the former, can, I believe, occur as a passing phase in families which are not permanent battlefields or prison-camps and that they occur when one parent elects, for whatever reason, to enforce his or her will ruthlessly in respect of some particular item of domestic discipline and are resolved when the other parent intervenes and calls him or her to order—'Don't you think you're being a little hard, darling?' is the standard English middle class phrase for dealing with such contingencies; and also that nightmares induced by a child's dread of being overwhelmed by its own feelings, although indicating that the child is likely to grow up alienated from itself, may also cease as the child grows older and acquires greater freedom and a more sophisticated repertoire of defensive manœuvres. Compare the not uncommon childhood nightmare of being overwhelmed by a tidal wave with the adult dream about a tidal wave which I quoted at the end of my section on anxious dreams. This was dreamt by a highly successful intellectual.*

Dreams of the Alienated

In this section I shall describe a number of types of dreams dreamt by people who are out of touch with themselves, and

* For evidence that in the last two paragraphs I have not been riding a private hobby horse and that there are, indeed, families in which the rigidity and unimaginativeness of both parents, or more usually of one parent coupled with the absence or weakness of the other, drives the children into situations in which their autonomy is at risk and the only escape is withdrawal into the privacy of mental illness, see the work of Bateson[25], Laing[26], Bowlby[27] and numerous papers in the American journal, *Family Process*. I must add that these paragraphs are based on impressions gained during the analysis of severely ill adult patients and not on direct experience with children —nor on families I have lived in or known personally.

who are engaged in one or other of the manœuvres open to people so placed, or rather unplaced: looking for themselves (the quest for an identity that was so fashionable in the 1950s and 1960s), trying to pass off a false self as a real one, resisting the incursions of their real selves, recapturing the state of affairs that existed prior to their original discovery of themselves as separate entities, and adopting an ironical or despairing stance of acceptance of their alienation. To people who are not and never have been alienated these dreams will have a peculiar ring, since they call into question some of the most elemental premises on which most people build their lives; that they know who they are, that they sometimes feel at home in the world, that the truth can be discovered.

The typical, or rather prototypical, dream of a person who is looking for himself is that of being asked by some stranger who he is, failing to find an answer or giving some answer that is puzzling or ambiguous. For instance, a woman dreamt that a policeman asked her to show him her identity card. When she did so, she was embarrassed to discover that it gave her name as 'hysteria'. Another woman, a doctor, dreamt that she was looking for her own case history and found it in a sealed envelope at the bottom of a pile of professional papers.

An example of a dream of a person who is trying to pass off a false self as a real one was provided by a young man, who had good grounds for supposing that he was the only bearer of his surname, which sounded rather distinguished. He dreamt that the butler of a fictitious Duke told him, rather snootily, that his surname was not one with which His Grace was familiar. He awoke with the retort on his lips that there must be many surnames in the world with which the Duke had yet to acquaint himself. The impossible architectural dreams of the American who passed himself off as more English than the English, quoted earlier in this book, belong in the same group.

People who devote themselves to resisting the incursion of their real selves not uncommonly dream of impending catastrophes, of countries just about to be overrun by invading armies, of air-raids, of nuclear missiles which fail to reach their target, of Martian space-ships on course towards the earth. Similiar delusions preoccupy the waking thoughts of schizophrenics, who explore the furthest reaches of alienation but rarely return to tell their tale.

Very rarely people may dream that the catastrophe has occurred, that the world is devasted, the sedge is withered and the birds have ceased to sing. These dreams seem to occur in people who have concealed their alienation beneath a cloak of illusions and have then suffered extreme and sudden disillusionment. A literary example of such a dream is provided by Leopardi's poem 'Terror by Night', which describes a dream— which apparently he really did have—in which the moon falls out of sky and burns itself out in a field. Leopardi, who according to one of his biographers 'committed to his notebook one of the most terrible indictments ever penned by a son against his mother', had this dream during the year in which he suddenly lost his religious faith, suffered from temporary blindness and felt, he said, like a 'living corpse'. I have discussed this dream and another, dreamt many years ago by a patient of mine, of the moon falling out of the sky into a dustbin in a paper entitled 'On Idealization, Illusion, and Catastrophic Disillusion'.[28]

Although dreams expressing wishes to abrogate alienation by recapturing the sense of oneness with the world and the mother are common, at any rate among people who enter psychotherapy, one kind of dream in this category is of particular interest. These are dreams which appear to be projected onto a screen or backcloth or in which the dream consists of a white or blank screen on which nothing is projected. Such dreams led the American analyst Lewin[29] to postulate that all dreams are projected onto a dream screen which is only occasionally visible, and to interpret the screen as a symbol of both sleep and the maternal breast. Later workers have doubted whether a dream screen is a component of all dreams and have suggested instead that dreams consisting of or including a screen only occur in people who are abandoning a schizoid state of withdrawal and entering, or teetering on the edge of, a manic state. Pure screen dreams seem to symbolize a state of ecstatic fusion with the breast, in which all wishes are imagined to be being satisfied by union with a pure, unblemished, perfect object.

A patient of mine, a man in his forties, once dreamt: 'it felt as though you had taken me under your wing. There was nothing to see in the dream at all. It was like a white sheet.' He then went on to say that he had had this dream three times during the same night, which had been the best night's sleep he could remember and that he had seen white sheets of light during his previous analytical session. A week or so later he again dreamt of a 'canvas, or perhaps a cinema screen, which was somehow also the walls of your consulting room. On it were depicted all the things I wanted to tell you when you got back from holiday.' It would seem that this man was trying to persuade himself that analytical treatment is a more blissful, enfolding experience than it in fact is. Although he dreamt that I took him under my wing and vouchsafed him a deep, satisfying sleep, in reality I went on holiday and left him to fend for himself.

In view of the fact that visions of pure light and moments of positively perceived nothingness occur in the *via negativa* of the mystics, and that Freud interpreted mystical states and oceanic feelings as phantasies of fusion with the breast, it seems likely that there is some connection between screen dreams and mystical experiences. R. C. Zaehner in his book *Mysticism: Sacred and Profane* distinguished between true mystical experiences which lead to 'sobriety' and false ones which lead to 'drunkenness' and are a form of madness, specifically mania.[31]

Ironic or despairing acceptance of alienation is expressed in the following two dreams, both dreamt by men who were familiar with current theories of alienation and who were, I think, mocking themselves for their tendency to reject the simple in favour of the difficult. One dreamt that he had joined an exclusive club, all the private rooms of which had notices on their doors saying 'Visitors Only', thereby representing himself as a member of an élite of outsiders and loners. The other dreamt that he noticed in the window of an antique shop an old book which he knew contained the Truth. On inquiring inside he was told that the book was the only known copy of an otherwise unknown work of Immanuel Kant and that it was written in a language no-one could understand.

Dreams of the Blind

The blind dream, but if they have never been sighted, their dreams lack visual imagery. Those who have lost their sight use visual imagery in their dreams if they can still picture things in their minds eye while awake. Three men who had been blind for 3, 10 and 15 years respectively all reported that they still saw things in their dreams, but two others, who had been blind for 30 and 40 years, reported that they no longer did. The former three all had rapid eye movements while dreaming, while the latter two did not.[32]

These observations suggest that dreaming is not essentially a visual activity even though to the sighted it appears to be, and support the idea that dreaming is imaginative activity as it manifests itself in sleep—the images used by imagination being of necessity those made available to it by sensation and memory.

I have included this section to substantiate a remark I made in a footnote to Chapter 3 (page 42) and to answer one of the first questions about dreams asked by people who become curious about them.

Punning Dreams

Dreams which exploit the fact that words may have more than one meaning or that words with the same sound may have different meanings, are not uncommon. Freud[33] cites a dream in which the dreamer was being kissed in an automobile; 'He went on at once to give me the interpretation, which I myself would never have guessed: namely that it meant auto-erotism.' Ella Sharpe[34] quotes a patient who dreamt 'Iona Cathedral' and another who dreamt of a courtyard and then went on to describe how she had got caught in an enclosed garden and had had to climb out over a spiked wall; as Ella Sharpe points out, this dream expresses anxiety about courting. After suffering a fracture of the penis—not as disastrous an event as it sounds—a patient of mine dreamt that a potted cyclamen fell to the ground, broke and then burst into flower. The sickly man was not emasculated but flourishing.

The punning possibilities of place-names are often exploited in dreams. Bournemouth may be the mother's genitals, since it is the mouth from which one was born, or it may be death, which is that bourne from which no traveller returns. Abyssinia may be visited in a dream, its attraction being that it is an abyss of sin. In pre-permissive days, when virginity was still prized, male dreamers sometimes went to Maidenhead.

Punning dreams are of some slight theoretical interest for three reasons, First, they reveal, as waking puns do too, the existence of phonetic connections between ideas and images which cut across their rational, logical connections. Reason and education insist that words have a prescribed meaning and that trains of thought should not jump across from one track to another. There is, as a result, something mildly subversive about punning, which cocks a snook at the established order of thought by bringing together momentarily meanings which reason says should be kept apart. Freud's assertion that he would never have guessed the pun on 'auto' is in line with his lack of sympathy with surrealist art, which sought to use his own science in a similarly subversive way. And since we all hear words for several years before we can read and see them, and must during these years hear many words used by grown-ups without knowing what they mean, the phonetic ramifications and private associations of many words must ante-date our knowledge of their agreed public meaning. For instance, a child was long puzzled by his parents' habit of shutting doors to keep giraffes out; he knew they lived in Africa not in England, and only when he had a fever and became temporarily sensitive to draughts did he discover that draughts and giraffes are different words and things.

So since dreaming is a private mode of communication between different parts of the self, the phonetic, preliterate connections between words, which are suppressed and ignored in waking speech, can be used freely in dreams, producing results which, when transcribed into waking discursive language, give the appearance of being puns.

Secondly, the fact that dreaming can utilize phonetic similarities and individually acquired connections between words is incompatible with the idea that dreams are manifestations of the unconscious, which is by definition innocent of words and language, and is evidence in support of the idea that dreams are—or on occasion can be—creations of the whole self. Or perhaps better, it is incompatible with the classical Freudian conception that the mind is divided into two parts, one of which, the id, lacks words while the other, the ego, is structured by them, and supports the idea that verbal and sensational 'thing' imagery are inextricably intertwined; that, indeed, words are not entities apart from and added to sensational images, but are themselves sensational images in the first instance auditory and concrete and then later visual and more or less abstract.

Thirdly, punning dreams are incompatible with the idea that dream imagery is a universal language which exists independently of the dreamer's social, cultural and linguistic equipment. When Jung dreamt that Liverpool was a pool of life, he was not tapping his collective unconscious, but drawing on, and, one suspects, showing off his knowledge of English.

Recurrent Dreams

Many, perhaps most, people have a dream which recurs, more or less unaltered, intermittently over the years. Typically such dreams are of sitting an examination, rushing to catch a train, finding an unknown room in one's house, travelling towards a city, being threatened by a tidal wave, or of violence occurring at some distance from oneself. When describing such dreams, people usually emphasize the similarity of each dream to its predecessors, but in therapy both patient and therapist tend to become more interested in the differences between the dreams, which can often be seen to form a developing series. For instance, the location, shape and contents of the unknown room may become progressively clearer, or the violence may come ever closer.

Recurrent dreams indicate the existence of an unsolved problem, the extent to which the dreams remain unaltered indicating the extent to which the dreamer is failing to solve it. In other words, a recurrent dream represents the posing of a problem and changes in it represent the gradual emergence of a solution—or, occasionally, the threat of being overwhelmed by a problem which has previously been ignored. A man dreamt recurrently that he was trying unsuccessfully to get through to his father's house. During therapy, he dreamt successively that he was approaching his father's house, that he had entered it, that he was in his father's study which was occupied by someone else, that he found a room which he at first thought was his own but turned out to be his brother's, and finally that he found a room in his father's house which was his own.

Examination Dreams

Dreams in which the dreamer is about to sit an examination which he in fact took years ago are not uncommon. They almost always invoke an examination which the dreamer in fact passed and can therefore be interpreted as self-reassuring— if, despite the anxiety you felt then, you passed that test, you can pass the forthcoming one.

Examination dreams may also hinge on the fact that in modern society examinations, for the professional classes at least, are *rites de passage* by which people pass from student to adult status. As a result people who, for whatever reason, do not feel they have grown up despite having passed the appropriate examinations, may recurrently dream that they still have to take the examination that they have in fact taken and passed. Dreams of taking, passing or failing driving tests can be similarly interpreted.

Physical Illness and Dreams

Both Aristotle and Hippocrates believed in the existence of 'prodromal' dreams occurring just before a physical illness declared itself, and explained them by asserting that dreams could magnify sensations, so that, for instance, bladder disease might be heralded by a dream of springs, or lung disease by a dream of being suffocated. This idea survived until the rise of scientific medicine and does not strike contemporary analysts and dream laboratory workers as absurd, though I know of no convincing instance of an analyst having diagnosed a physical illness solely by means of dream interpretation.

Ella Sharpe [35] reported the following dream of a woman who was continuing to work despite extreme lassitude: she was clinging with all her might to a window ledge and then, finally exhausted, she fell to the ground. Two days later she fainted and was found to be suffering from a long-standing bladder infection. To my mind this dream is better interpreted as a warning to stop driving herself too hard and as a wish to give up doing so than as an indication that she knew that she was physically ill. The text of the dream contains nothing that could be interpreted as evidence of unconscious knowledge of her bladder infection.

Ella Sharpe also quotes an impressive dream dreamt by an 81-year-old woman three days before her death. 'I saw all my sicknesses gathered together and as I looked they were no longer sicknesses but roses and I knew the roses would be planted and that they would grow.'

Imperative Dreams

Dreams in which the dreamer is commanded or exhorted by a voice, usually not his own, are common. By far the commonest dream command or exhortation is 'Wake Up' but the call may be professional, gnomic or absurd, e.g. 'Catalogue this, please', dreamt by a librarian, 'Go and find Maria Athenas', 'Fetch the Squigger.'

Although dreams of being woken up by a voice saying 'wake up' lend themselves to an obvious common-sense interpretation, it is my impression that they only occur in people who are withdrawn and introverted and do indeed need to wake up, metaphorically speaking, to the world around them—and in sleeping beauties who are waiting for someone to awaken them.

CHAPTER 6

Sleep and the Physiology of Dreams

Sleep

All mammals, birds and reptiles sleep and it must presumably have beneficial effects which outweigh such disadvantages as the fact that during it vigilance is reduced and vulnerability to attack is increased. It seems to be generally assumed that, among the higher mammals at least, the brain is the organ which requires sleep most. As a result most research on sleep concentrates on the changes in the activity of the brain that occur during it, some of which are reflected in electrical activity which can be measured and recorded by an electro-encephalogram. This can be attached to the scalp without injury or discomfort and, as a result, it is possible to record the brain-waves of waking and sleeping animals and human volunteers without difficulty. In 1953 Aserinsky and Kleitman[1] discovered that sleep consisted of two qualitatively distinct phases, during one of which people dream and during the other of which they do not. Since then an enormous amount of research on the physiology of sleep and dreams has been conducted, mostly in the United States, leading to a plethora of facts without, however, generating any generally accepted hypotheses about their function.

However, all researchers into the electrophysiology of sleep seem to agree that there are two kinds of sleep, normal or orthodox sleep, which can itself be sub-divided into various stages or depths of sleep, and paradoxical sleep, during which the sleeper appears to be in some ways deeply asleep and in other ways lightly asleep. During paradoxical sleep most of the muscles of the body are deeply relaxed but nonetheless grimaces and rapid movements of the eyes occur and individual limbs may move suddenly and briefly. It seems that most if not all dreams occur during the paradoxical phase of sleep, that the rapid eye movements are the dreamer as it were following the dream events in his mind's eye, and that the facial and limb movements correspond to the feelings he is having and the actions he is performing during the dream.

So far as is known all mammals, other than perhaps ruminants, demonstrate paradoxical as well as orthodox sleep, and it is therefore tempting though unscientific to assume that they also dream. There also appears to be a need for paradoxical sleep, since animals and human beings who are deprived of it 'catch up on it' when they are allowed to sleep normally again.

Freud's writings on dreams take sleep for granted, merely assuming that there is a physiological need for sleep and that the function of dreaming is to prevent repressed wishes from disturbing it. The work of later analysts, notably Lewin,[2] suggests, however, that sleep may itself on occasion acquire symbolic meaning, the state of being asleep representing fusion with the mother's breast. In people in whom this symbolic equation is operative, excessive sleeping may constitute an enactment of regression to the breast, insomnia may be due to ambivalence towards the breast, and the ability largely to dispense with sleep, as occurs in mania, may be due to the presence of a phantasy or unconscious belief that one has fused with the breast and therefore no longer requires sleep. Experimental research suggests, however, that there is a basic, actual, non-symbolic need for sleep and that attempts to dispense with it or to deprive others of it are doomed to failure—and that people who claim never to sleep are deceiving themselves, as are also those who claim never to dream.

However, research also suggests that people who are worried and depressed, 'who tend to feel their problems rather than to push them aside'[3] need more sleep than conventional 'pre-programmed' people who run along smooth, familiar tracks, and that the extra requirement is specifically for paradoxical dream sleep. The implication of these observations is that sleep, and particularly dream sleep, has a restorative function after anxiety or stress, and perhaps after any waking 'reprogramming' or 'rearrangement'. Hartmann also mentions that he knows five physicians who report a decrease in their sleep requirements following successful psychoanalytical treatment, and that he has not heard of any cases of change in the opposite direction.

The discovery of the existence of paradoxical sleep has led to the suggestion that Freud's idea that we dream in order to preserve sleep needs reversing, and that on the contrary we sleep in order to dream. But this re-formulation cannot be quite right either. Paradoxical sleep occupies about half of the sleeping time of newborn infants and about a fifth of the sleeping time of adults, which leaves between a half and four-fifths of our sleeping time unaccounted for. So it would seem that the function or functions of sleep, which we suppose on general grounds to be concerned with recuperation, restoration, growth, integration, programming and re-programming, must be of two kinds, one of which requires dreaming, the other of which requires dreamlessness.

The famous nineteenth century neurologist Hughlings Jackson (1835–1911) suggested that sleep fulfils the dual functions of sweeping away unnecessary memories from the previous day and of consolidating or maintaining more necessary ones, an idea which seems to be being confirmed by much of the recent research. He also held that 'manifestly new, although evanescent combinations are made during dreaming; but I contend that permanent rearrangements (Internal Evolutions) are made during so-called dreamless sleep.' Perhaps this will prove true too.

Finally, the fact that we spend up to four-fifths of sleeping life totally unconscious, not even dreaming, raises problems about the basis of our sense of possessing a continuous identity, since it suggests that at every awakening our identity is reconstituted from its biological matrix—an idea much harder to apprehend than that our identity is sustained throughout sleep by dreaming.

Forgetting and Remembering Dreams

Since the physiological evidence suggests that we all dream for about a fifth of the time that we are asleep, the majority of dreams dreamt must be forgotten. Indeed, since some people claim never to dream, it must be possible for people to forget all their dreams. On the face of it, therefore, the fact that some dreams are remembered and others are forgotten, and that some people remember dreams frequently, some people remember dreams seldom, and yet others remember them never, constitutes a problem.

Curiously enough, this problem is almost always raised in connection with forgetting dreams, the tacit assumption being that dreams are experiences analogous to events or happenings, that events are normally remembered, and that it must therefore require some special explanation to account for forgetting dream events. On this view of the matter, forgetting dreams is as remarkable as, and is the same kind of phenomenon as, forgetting the whole of one's childhood, losing one's memory, or forgetting about things that are of importance in one's everyday life—all of which are instances of forgetting that are, in principle, pathological, since they impoverish one's sense of self and interfere with one's capacity to function efficiently; there is obviously something amiss if one has forgotten one's origins, if one has lost one's memory and no longer knows who one is, or if one fails to remember things that one has to do or facts that have a bearing on one's life. So, if dreams really were events, forgetting them would be a form of amnesia, a forgetting of what in health would be remembered, and is due to some conflict, inhibition or repression which prevents the emergence into consciousness of wishes, thoughts and recollections that would disturb the dreamer's waking equanimity and received conception of himself.

Now, although the forgetting of many dreams must be explicable in this way—just as many instances of forgetting things in waking life are patently due to the wish to forget than, e.g. forgetting to pay bills, to keep dreaded appointments, forgetting the names of people one dislikes, or wishes to snub, or who remind one of events of which one is ashamed—consideration of the nature and function of memory and of the quantitative relationship existing between the past and the present* will show that it cannot possibly be true that in a state of ideal health people would be able to remember every thought and image of which they have ever been conscious, whether in their sleep or while awake,—and that the assumption that they could is an example of misapplying ideas derived from pathology.

According to biological and neurological theory, the function of memory is to enable each organism or individual to base his actions on a wider range of experience than would be available to him if he had no memory; to enable him to interpret the present in terms of past experience and to make decisions which take account of the past as well as of the immediate present. And an efficient memory is one which makes available to its owner information relevant to his present and future without distracting him by irrelevancies. In other words,

* Since there is so much more of the past than there is of the present and remembering is an activity that takes time and can itself be remembered, there is something absurd about the idea that all experiences could be remembered in the form in which they were experienced. Recall would take up more time than was available for it and infinite regresses (remembering oneself remembering oneself remembering . . .) would clutter up the system. What in fact happens is, of course, that all experiences, including events, imaginings, reflections and dreams are subject to a continuous process of selection, abstraction, generalization, distillation. When Proust set out on his *A la Recherche du Temps Perdu*, what he discovered was not a serial account of the time he had lost (not forgotten (*oublié*), a point which the English translation, Remembrance of Things Past, misses) but a distillation of it.[5]

when memory is functioning harmoniously, information (memories) relevant to work will be available when working, information relevant to home will be available at home, information relevant to childhood will be available when in the company of children, information relevant to food will be available when hungry, and so on—and information which would be distracting will be unavailable.*

It follows from this that memory is not, as it were, an inbuilt audio-visual tape of one's past thoughts and experiences, all parts of which should ideally be instantly available, but a selective process by which the present self is continuously fed with relevant memories from its past and protected from distraction and confusion by some barrier to remembering the irrelevant. It follows from this too that there are three categories of past experience that can loosely be described as forgotten; those which will never have any bearing on the present and never are or need be retrieved, e.g. half-formed thoughts which never crystallize out into a definite idea or decision, or the intermediate stages of a calculation the final result of which may be retrievable; those which remain dormant or latent because situations on which they might have bearing are not being presently encountered, e.g. a language once learnt but not at present being used; and those which do have bearing on the present but are rendered unavailable by conflict, inhibition and repression, e.g. memories of childhood events which have a bearing on aspects of the self with which the present self is not in contact, and, more dramatically, fugue states (loss of memory) in which the individual forgets who he is.

What I am suggesting, then, is that dreams are forgotten or remembered for exactly the same reasons as waking thoughts are forgotten or remembered, and that the idea that there is

* If this were not so—if remembering and forgetting were not dependent on the subject's set and setting—doctors and dentists would be distracted by professional considerations while making love, and psychoanalysts would be confused by recollections of patients other than the one they are with.

THE INNOCENCE OF DREAMS

anything peculiar about many of them being forgotten derives from two sources: the assumption that they are events subjectively endowed with objective reality, which, if they were, would make it surprising that dreams with an exotic content could be forgotten; and a misguided view of memory as an unselective, instantly replayable tape of all one's past experiences, thoughts and imaginings.

Dreams, then, may be forgotten because the thoughts contained within them never crystallized out into a message definite enough to be remembered, because they formed part of a 're-arrangement', meditation or conflict that once completed or resolved never needs to be remembered, because they appear to have no relevance to the present in which the dreamer lives, which in cultures that deny meaning to dreams and set little value on subjectivity may for all practical purposes be true, or because the message they contain is too disturbing to be remembered.

In contrast, dreams may be remembered because the message contained within them may be sensed to be too important to be forgotten—Wilkie Collins's novel *Basil*[6] contains a beautiful example of such a dream, which was, probably, actually dreamt by Collins[7]—because the dreamer is living a life in which it is assumed that dreams do have relevance, e.g. is spending his nights in a dream laboratory or temple (see Chapter 7) or his days on an analyst's couch, because he is involved in some private voyage of self-exploration, or because he is finding his waking life so boring that he invokes imagination or fancy to entertain himself. In this last case, dreaming becomes nocturnal day-dreaming.

For obvious reasons I cannot give examples of dreams that were forgotten before they were told to me—and if a patient tells me a dream and later forgets it, I, if I remember it, can remind him of it and it ceases to be forgotten. I cannot remember any patient ever repudiating a dream that he has forgotten and I have remembered, which suggests that absence of feedback plays an important part in the 'normal' forgetting of dreams.

It is, however, a myth that analysts remember all their patients' dreams—or all of their own. Dreams which never acquire relevance to the present, because neither patient nor analyst discerns their meaning, tend to be forgotten; as also do dreams that lose relevance because the problem or conflict they deal with has been resolved. And presumably analysts can forget dreams of their patients that contain messages too disturbing for them themselves to remember. All the dreams cited in this book were, however, remembered by their dreamers for long enough to be told to me, and have been remembered by me for long enough to be quoted here.

Earlier in this book I mentioned that it is possible to dream about anxiety, as opposed to dreaming anxiously (see p. 109). Similarly, it is possible to dream about remembering without actually remembering anything. A woman who had great difficulty in remembering either her dreams or her childhood, some aspects of which did seem to have a bearing on her present problems, dreamt that after going through a tunnel and through a door usually kept locked she came to a library full of books, only to discover that the card index was in disarray and that she could not, therefore, locate the books she was looking for. This dream seems to me to illuminate research done at the dream laboratory in Edinburgh[8] which suggests that convergent thinkers who specialize in analytical thinking are less likely to remember their dreams than are divergent thinkers, who are more imaginative and able to deal with the non-rational, who are not thrown by the absence of categories and guide-lines, symbolized in my patient's dream by the card index.

Dream Deprivation

Since most if not all dreams occur in the so-called paradoxical phase of sleep, characterized by rapid eye movements, it should be possible to deprive experimental subjects and animals of the opportunity to dream by awakening them from sleep the moment rapid eye movements begin, and to observe the effects of such deprivation on their waking behaviour and on their later periods of sleep. To this end human beings, presumably all volunteers, have been deprived of paradoxical sleep for up to six days, and cats, presumably not volunteers, have been deprived of it for up to seventy days.

The most consistent finding in such dream deprivation experiments has been that the amount of paradoxical sleep, and therefore presumably dreaming, increases enormously during the sleeps immediately following cessation of the deprivation, which suggests that people and animals deprived of the opportunity to dream 'catch up on' their lost dream sleep as soon as they can. In view of the fact that psychoanalytical and psychiatric thinking tends to liken dreams to hallucinations and dreaming to psychosis, it had been surmised that dream deprivation might induce waking hallucinations or other 'psychotic' symptoms, but this seems not to be so. People and animals deprived of paradoxical sleep become 'hyper-excitable', but do not hallucinate, and, according to Dement (1968), 'Although a restorative process and, by inference, a need for REM sleep is suggested, no study has shown that REM deprivation has significant functional consequences for the waking life of human subjects.'[9]

Dreams of Animals

Since the discovery that dreaming occurs, mostly if not entirely, during the paradoxical phase of sleep and is associated with rapid eye movements, it has become plausible to suppose that those animals which both sleep and display bursts of rapid eye movements intermittently while doing so, dream, and that those animals which do not sleep or do not display bursts of rapid eye movements during sleep, do not.

Nothing resembling sleep has been observed in fishes, so presumably they do not dream. Reptiles and birds sleep, but rapid eye movements 'as a clearly recognizable entity' do not occur, so presumably they do not dream. However, all mammals, with the possible exception of ungulates, both sleep and display rapid eye movements while doing so, so presumably mammals do dream. (If it really is true that ungulates do not have a paradoxical phase of sleep and hence do not dream, a ready evolutionary explanation of this anomaly is to hand; hoofed animals depend for their survival on their capacity for rapid flight from predators and the bodily immobilization that characterizes the paradoxical phase of sleep would therefore deprive them of their major self-protective device.)

Since, however, all mammals other than man lack the capacity for symbolic thought, their dreams must consist of fairly simple imagery related to their basic drives, i.e. food, sex, flight, fight and submission. Jouvet (1965) claims that by destroying a nucleus in the midbrain it is possible to prepare cats which retain the capacity to move during the paradoxical phase of sleep. Such cats appear 'to stare fearfully at invisible objects' and to 'react to an hallucinated enemy'.[10]

Colour in Dreams

If asked, most people can tell one whether their dreams are coloured or in black and white, but dreamers usually only spontaneously mention the presence or absence of colour in any particular dream if either (1) the coloration or lack of colour is uncharacteristic and unlike the kind of dream to which they are accustomed, or (2) if the colour of some particular image appears to be a significant detail about it. The colour of a person, or of his clothes, may refer to his name—e.g. Brown, Green, Black—or to some mental attribute which can be symbolized by colour, e.g. green for callow, blue for cold or sad, red for angry or embarrassed.

The colour of any object appearing in a dream may indicate that it is being used as a symbol for a body surface, fluid or product—hence brown for faeces or for pigmented skin, white for unpigmented skin or for milk or semen, red for blood, yellow for urine.

Attempts have been made to show that dreaming in colour or not is of psychological significance, and that, for instance, only exhibitionists habitually dream in colour, but workers at the Institute of Dream Research, Santa Cruz, California,[11] have admitted themselves defeated in their attempts to determine the significance of colour in dreams by comparing 'chromatic' and 'achromatic' dreams. They conclude that colour in dreams yields no information about the personality of the dreamer.

Experiments reported by Berger[12] suggest that most people dream in colour most of the time, which is also my impression. It is also my impression that consistent dreaming in colourless imagery occurs only in people, who, are inhibited and chronically mildly depressed, but that consistent dreaming in 'glorious technicolor' with exaggeratedly bright colours occurs only in people who, in waking life, have something strident and forced about them. In view of the likelihood that most people dream in colour most of the time, it is, perhaps, relevant that I have met people, both professionally and socially, who assert in loud voices that they *always* dream in colour in tones that imply that it is, they believe, evidence of some special sensibility. They are the same people as those who have migraines and nightmares when we lesser mortals have headaches and anxiety dreams.

The intensity, or lack of intensity, of colour in dreams is, I would imagine, correlated with the degree of vividness of mental imagery in waking life, though I have not encountered any literature on the subject.

Erections in Dreams

Following a lead given by two papers published in Germany in 1944 and 1947, Fisher, Gross and Zuch[13] observed 17 male subjects for 27 nights and discovered that during 95 per cent of their periods of dream sleep their penises were erect, the erections beginning at or shortly before the onset of rapid eye movements and subsiding in 'close temporal relationship' to their end. If this observation proved generally true, it would mean that men have erections whenever they dream. As Fisher, Gross and Zuch themselves point out, it is remarkable that this correlation 'has not been discovered throughout the history of mankind'. Similar observations have been made on male laboratory animals but nothing equivalent so far as I can discover, on women.

If this observation proves to be a fact, and not an artifact instigated by the laboratory equipment attached to the volunteer subjects' members, it should, one feels, be significant, but in what way it is hard to say. Fisher et al. are clear that it has nothing to do with sexual deprivation nor with filling of the bladder, but they seem to be in uncertainty as whether to regard it as of physiological or psychological significance, i.e. whether to regard it as part of the physiology of dream sleep or as evidence of regression to some 'primitive level of auto-erotic organisation of penile sensation characteristic of early infancy'.

Although the significance of this observation is obscure, it is, however, of some general interest that experimental work of this kind is being done—and was being done, and presumably financed, in Germany during the closing stages of the last war. And it is an item of which no contemporary writer on dreams could afford to appear to be ignorant.

CHAPTER 7

Dream Incubation and Visitations

Culture Pattern Dreams and Dream Incubation

Anthropologists divide dreams into two kinds; 'individual' or 'free' dreams, which reflect the dreamer's everyday life and preoccupations, and 'culture pattern' or 'official' dreams, (Lincoln[1] and Malinowski[2] respectively), which are prescribed by custom and induced by special rituals. Nothing analogous to 'culture pattern' dreams exists in contemporary Western societies, since dreaming plays no part in any of our social or religious ceremonies or in any of our techniques for making decisions, predicting the future or diagnosing illnesses.

In ancient times, however, things were very different. In ancient Egypt and in classical Greece and Rome dream interpretation was practised by oneirocrits, who were priests and physicians, and temples existed in which clients would seek advice, prophecies and diagnoses. In such temples, of which there are said to have been more than three hundred active in Greece and the Roman Empire in the second century A.D., dream incubation was practised. The client or patient fell asleep in the temple and dreamt a dream in which the God of the temple appeared and indicated what action the dreamer should follow or what medecine he should take.

Unless these temples were all fraudulent and the clients only pretended to dream—which is unlikely—dreams following dream incubation must have been 'culture pattern' dreams in Lincoln's sense, the theophanies occurring in them being evoked by the action of the atmosphere created by the temples' architecture and fittings—and the liturgical bedside manners of the priest—on the dreamer's store of imagery, which must presumably always have included an image of the deity being consulted.

Dream temples and dream incubation seem not to have survived the establishment of christendom, but medieval and, indeed, seventeenth century ideas on dreams allowed for the possibility of dreams in which a priest, a guardian angel, or a God appeared and offered the dreamer advice or information. For instance Sir Thomas Browne (1605–82), the physician and author of the *Religio Medici*, believed that guardian spirits 'may sometimes order our dreams: and many strange hints, instigations, or discourses, which are so amazing unto us, may arise from such foundations.' But he also thought that 'the phantasms of sleep do commonly walk in the great road of natural and animal dreams, wherein the thoughts and actions of the day are acted over and echoed in the night.'

But if people really did have dreams in which, so it seemed to them, supernatural beings appeared and offered them advice or information, these too would have to be classified as culture pattern dreams.

So far as I can discover, the European pre-scientific view of dreams was not specifically Christian but rather a licensed or tolerated survival from pagan classical times and was based on the pre-Cartesian assumption that a mental image can be something more than a representation or (in the modern sense) symbol of its referent; it could be it or 'correspond' to it in some real sense. Given this assumption about the relationship between images and objects, there was nothing superstitious or irrational about interpreting dreams in terms of the real presence or true intervention of God, saints and angels—or of the Devil and demons. Indeed the occurrence of their images, whether in dreams or in waking life, was, according to the Ontological Argument*, evidence in favour of their existence.

Two of the most widely read scholarly works on dreams in

* The Ontological Argument, first elaborated by St Anselm, asserts that the existence of the idea of God necessarily implies His objective existence. Not surprisingly, it is repudiated by most modern philosophers and by empiricists, and particularly if applied to ideas other than God, it can lead to absurdities.

the Middle Ages were those of Macrobius and Artemidorus, neither of whom were Christians.

Macrobius, who lived around 400 A.D., wrote a commentary on Cicero's *The Dream of Scipio*, in which he classified dreams into five types, two insignificant and three significant. The insignificant types were nightmares, which he attributed to 'vexations similar to those that disturb [the dreamer] during the day', and *phantasma*, by which he appears to have meant hypnagogic hallucinations occurring while falling asleep. Nightmares and phantasma were deemed by Macrobius to be insignificant and unworthy of interpretation because they have no prophetic significance, being merely the result and reflection of the dreamer's everyday preoccupations. His three significant types of dream were *somnia* or enigmatic dreams, which 'conceal(s) with strange shapes and veil(s) with ambiguity the true meaning of the information being offered', *visiones*, which 'actually come(s) true', and *oracula*, in which 'a parent, or a pious or revered man or a priest, or even a God'[3] appears and gives advice or information. In a culture which not only admitted the possibility of enigmas, visions, and oracula but also, being theocentric and theocratic, held that they were the only dreams of any real importance, the others being mere vexations, there must have been strong pressure to persuade oneself that some at least of one's dreams were visitations; just as modern secular post-Freudian man is under pressure to discover that his dreams are replete with sexual symbolism. Using the phrase in an extended sense, dreams cannot but be culture pattern dreams; their images can only derive from two sources, the dreamer's body and the imagery and iconography of the culture that surrounds him, and their interpretation can only be in terms of the ideas, explicit and implicit, prevalent and fashionable within it. One can, indeed, conceive of society itself as a temple in which dreams are incubated by the symbolic atmosphere created by its priests and physicians.

Artemidorus of Daldis was a Greek physician who practised in Italy in the second century A.D. His *Oneirocritica* is held to be the most important book on dreams to survive from classical times and is apparently based on a life-time spent visiting incubation temples, interviewing other dream-interpreters and collecting old manuscripts. It consists of five books, three of which he published, while the other two were reserved for his son, also a dream interpreter and also called Artemidorus, to use privately in his practice.

Artemidorus distinguished five types of dreams; symbolic dreams such as Pharaoh's dream of the fat and lean kine; day-time visions; oracular dreams containing divine revelations; fantasies or undisguised wish-fulfilling dreams; and nightmares. He also distinguished between *insomnium* dreams which were affected by the dreamer's physical state and daytime concerns, and *somnium* dreams which were allegorical and referred to future events.

He believed that interpretation of any particular dream was only possible if six facts were known about it: whether the events depicted in the dream were plausible or bizarre; whether they were approximately interconnected; whether they were customary for the dreamer; what events prior to the dream could have influenced it; and the dreamer's name and occupation.

According to his most recent English editor and translator,[4] Artemidorus hedged on whether dreams are messages from the Gods or individual, personal creations, but Ruth Padel,[5] reviewing this new translation in the *Times Literary Supplement*, asserts that he conformed to the Greek tradition of assuming without question that all human activity is both due entirely to the influence of the Gods and explicable in exclusively human terms.

E. R. Dodds, who unlike the present writer seems actually to have read the *Oneirocritica*, mentions in his essay Supernormal Phenomena in Classical Antiquity[6] that Artemidorus records ninety-five dreams allegedly collected by him from contemporaries and that in nine of these Gods appear to the dreamer. He also says that Artemidorus's list of symbols for women would be mostly acceptable to present-day psychoanalysts.

In view of the historical importance of the *Oneirocritica* and of the fact that Artemidorus believed that dreams could be wish-fulfilling, it is perhaps worth mentioning that the first edition of Freud's *Interpretation of Dreams* contained only one reference to the *Oneirocritica* in the main text—and one footnote referring to the prudery of the German translator who omitted to translate the chapter on sexual dreams. However, in later editions, between 1908 and 1914, Freud added four more references to Artemidorus.

God and Dreams

I, waking, called my dream to mind
Which to instruct me heaven designed.
Thomas Ken (1637–1711),
Bishop of Bath and Wells; hymn writer.

It is possible to believe that dreams have meaning and at the same time to believe that their meaning derives from someone or something other than oneself—one candidate for this other being God. Although it must be a rarity for anyone nowadays to believe, as Bishop Ken appears to have, that dreams are instructions from a transcendental God 'out there' or up in heaven, even today new theologians who define God as the Ground of our Being can regard dreams as messages from God.

Prior, however, to the scientific revolution that was already in progress during Bishop Ken's lifetime, it was widely if not universally believed that God—or in classical times the Gods—could participate in the formation of dreams. Indeed, since God was believed to be omnipresent, it was inconceivable that He should not be present in dreams; and, furthermore, since all meaning was ultimately generated by Him and everything that he created had meaning, dreams could not but contain messages from Him—even though Man's blindness and God's inscrutability might make it difficult if not impossible to de-cipher them. However medieval writers on dreams seem not only to have believed that some dreams were supernatural but even that a God could appear in a dream and offer advice, warnings or instructions.

It has been suggested by E. R. Dodds[7] that oracular dreams may be examples of culture-pattern dreams, and that people really did have such dreams at a time and in a culture which was patriarchal and authoritarian and conceived of all authority and morality as vested in persons and emanating from a God; whereas nowadays, when both the physical and the moral universe are conceived of abstractly and impersonally, people no longer do. It is, I hope, not altogether fanciful to point out that Bishop Ken's view of dreams is in a sense transitional. He does not dream that God appears and instructs him, he asserts as a matter of belief that his dream was designed in heaven to instruct him.

Over the years I have had several believing Christians, both Anglican and Catholic, as patients, but not one of them has ever reported a dream in which God has appeared; but three patients have reported to me childhood visions which a medi-eval theologian would, I believe, have diagnosed as oracula.

Visitations

A number of people are able to recall an experience in their childhood in which they were visited by some special being who blessed them, cursed them, advised them or called them. Typically, children who have such experiences treat them as intensely private and do not tell any grown-up about them until they themselves are grown up. Typically, too, they recognize during the experience that it is not explicable by common sense but do not categorize it as either craziness or as 'only' a dream.

In a religious setting visitations may be regarded as a natural occurrence, the special being may be identified as Christ, a saint or an angel—or as the Devil or a demon—and the message interpreted as a call to some special way of life.

In a secular setting, however, visitations have to be explained in psychological terms, as dialogues between the waking 'normal' self or ego and the wider Self speaking impersonally and authoritatively occurring under conditions in which the subject is partly awake and partly asleep; in the few cases of which I have detailed knowledge, the visited child was alone, in bed, in an unfamiliar room. Benign visitations seem to mark the achievement of a precocious self-awareness which sets the child apart from other children of his own age as possessing insight beyond his years, while malignant visitations seem to herald the onset of a severe neurosis. A woman who was visited by the Devil, whose blandishments she heroically resisted, spent much of her adult life under psychiatric treatment contending with the fact that as a child she had teetered on the edge of making hate, not love, the centre of her being.

Null visitations, which consign the child to limbo, can also occur. A seven-year-old girl was lying awake in a hotel bedroom while her father was visiting her mother in a maternity hospital. An old woman entered the room and walked towards the girl's bed seemingly about to say something to her. But she seemed to change her mind, turned round, and walked out of the room without having said anything at all.

Christ and Dreams

No dreams dreamt by Christ are recorded in the *New Testament*. This is in striking contrast to the fact that several dreams dreamt by Buddha and Mahomet are recorded and that much of the Koran was revealed to Mahomet in dreams. It is tempting to correlate the lack of any record of Christ's dreams with the fact that dream interpretation plays no part in Christian religious theory or practice. There are, however, Talmudic writings on dreams, and David Bakan in his *Freud and the Jewish Mystical Tradition*[8] has suggested that Freud was more influenced by them than is generally recognized or admitted.

CHAPTER 8

Reprise

Readers who have borne with me so far will appreciate that this book has two themes, not one.

The first, which constitutes its manifest content, is a contribution to oneirics, to the study of dreams considered as an ordinary part of everyday, or rather every night, life. To introduce this theme, I presented the two theories of dreams that arose within medicine at the beginning of this century and have enjoyed wide acceptance during the succeeding seventy-five years. I then went on to propose a third, imaginative theory of dreaming, one which, with two vital exceptions, bears a close resemblance to the traditional, literary—as opposed to the popular, superstitious—view of dreams.

The two exceptions are the importance I have attached to body symbolism in the formation of dream imagery and my assertion that the messages contained in dreams are concerned with the dreamer's biological destiny—with his inheritance, genetic and social, from his parents, with his survival as an autonomous self, with his recreation or continuation of himself as an actual or symbolic parent. These two ideas derive unequivocally from Freud, can indeed be construed as mere revisions or restatements of his theories, but they have the merit that they make it clear that sex in dreams—and in waking life too—is not 'something else besides', but an integral part of each individual's biological destiny, to use the most inclusive term possible to describe the whole life cycle of birth, growth, love, reproduction, ageing and death; a cycle which is destiny not career since it is determined not only by choice, decision, and will, but also by biological patterns that are inborn and ineluctable (e.g. innate vitality, temperament, aptitudes, age of onset of puberty and ageing) and by social considerations that are not of the individual's choice. We did not choose our parents, nor the culture into which we were born, nor the impact upon us of the various social, economic and intellectual movements at work within that culture.

Having proposed an imaginative theory of dreams, I then went on to describe how images derived from natural objects and artifacts interweave with those derived from the body to produce the symbols that appear in dreams, emphasizing largely because it has been too much neglected—the part played in this process by the literal language of words and the meta-phorical language of artifacts, i.e. by the public, social messages implicit in the clothes we wear, the houses we live in, the foods we cook, eat, and feed others with, and in our habits of speech.

Next I discussed various types of dreams. Some of these I included in order to answer questions that occur immediately to most people when they first become curious about dreams. Others were types of dreams with which many readers will be familiar, either because they have had such dreams themselves or have heard them recounted by others. Yet others were dis-cussed because they are of theoretical interest. Some of these, so far from having a familiar ring about them, will have seemed strange to some readers. Although everyone dreams and does so, I suggest, about the same basic theme, 'the fundamental and perennial interests of mankind', the imagery used to express this theme and the relationship maintained between the dream-ing and waking self vary so much from person to person, from culture to culture, that there is not and never could be any consensus of dreams. A dream, which may seem ordinary and natural to one person, may seem crazy and bizarre to another. Some readers will, I suspect, have felt surprised or even incredulous while reading about some of the dreams I have reported, while others will, I hope, have been reassured to discover that dreams they have had are not after all as peculiar as they imagined.

Although some readers may perhaps have felt that the

chapters on sleep and on culture pattern dreams were digressions, it was, I think, necessary to discuss the relationship between dreaming a subjective, psychological experience and sleep as observable, physiological activity, and between dreams as private, personal experience and the public culture which prescribes the kind of meaning with which they can be endowed and provides the 'not-self' contribution to the imagery of which they constituted.

It also seemed to be of some general interest to draw attention to a dialectical process that appears to be at work in Western culture's attitude towards dreams. First, dreams are taken seriously inasmuch as dream temples are maintained where dreams are interpreted on the assumption that they may throw light on the future. Then, they are ignored and consigned to limbo as irrational phenomena unworthy of serious consideration. Then they are treated seriously again, first on the assumption that they can throw light on the past of irrational disorders such as neuroses, and then later again, that is now, dream laboratories are maintained, in which research is conducted on the part played by dreaming in the individual's total adaptation to time; i.e. on the part played by dreaming in the process by which the individual assimilates the past which he has experienced, the present which he is experiencing, and the future which he anticipates he will experience.

The second, latent theme of this book is an exploration of the source or origin of creative, imaginative activity. Is it Freud's Id, Jung's Collective Unconscious, Groddeck's It, Coleridge's Imagination? Is it located in the body or in the mind, or in the self, and, if so, in what self? What is the relationship between the self that imagines and the self that wills? Does creative activity take place while awake, while dreaming, or even, perhaps, during dreamless sleep? The nearest I can get to answers to such questions will be found in the next chapter.

CHAPTER 9

Dreams and the Literary Imagination*

Throughout this book I have been maintaining the thesis that dreaming is better conceived as the form taken by the imagination during sleep than as an 'abnormal psychical phenomenon' analogous to the symptoms produced by neurotic conflict or the hallucinations of psychosis. In this, my last chapter I shall discuss some of the ways in which dreaming and the literary imagination resemble and differ from one another; and, more specifically, in what ways and to what extent Freudian theory is or is not applicable to the literary imagination. I shall open my argument by restating Freud's theory of the primary and secondary processes.

In Freud's view the most important, the most seminal, and the most revolutionary idea he ever had was that the human mind is capable of thinking in two different ways or modes; that there are, to use the title of one of his papers, 'two principles of mental functioning', one of which is characteristic of our waking life, the other characteristic of dreaming and neurotic symptom-formation; and that these two modes can be defined by presenting them in antithesis to one another, so that each can be conceived as possessing characteristics which are the opposite of the other,

Freud termed these two antithetical principles or modes the primary and secondary processes, the primary processes being those characteristic of our dream life, the secondary processes

* This chapter is based on, but not identical with, a lecture I gave at University College, London, on February 3rd, 1975, as part of the Freud Memorial Public Lectureship Programme 1974–5 and published in the *New York Review of Books* on April 3rd, 1975, under the title 'Freud and the Imagination'.

being those characteristic of our waking thought. The primary processes, in Freud's terminology, are condensation, by which mental images fuse with one another, and displacement, by which they replace and symbolize one another. Furthermore, the primary processes ignore opposites and the categories of space and time and are inherently wish-fulfilling. The secondary processes, on the other hand, respect the differences between images, obey the laws of grammar and formal logic, take cognisance of opposites and of the categories of space and time, and are adapted to the realities of the external world. To use a terminology Freud himself did not use, the primary processes are iconic and non-discursive, the secondary processes are verbal and discursive, the meaning of primary process utterances being only ascertainable by analysis and interpretation of the various condensations, displacements and symbolizations contained in the dream, the meaning of secondary process utterances being ascertainable by reference to the lexical and syntactical rules of the language which the waking speaker or writer is using. It was, furthermore, Freud's view that the primary processes in some sense come before the secondary processes—hence, of course, the nomenclature—and are, therefore, more infantile, more primitive and less adaptive than the secondary processes, which are learned during the course of each individual's development from being a primitive, phantasizing infant to a civilized, realistic, adapted adult.

Before proceeding to discuss in what way Freud's theory of the primary and secondary processes does or does not throw light on the literary imagination, it is necessary for me to make three comments on the theory itself and on the intellectual, cultural milieu within which Freud formulated it.

First, Freud unwittingly got himself involved in an inherently paradoxical activity when he tried to formulate in words the nature of a type of thinking which is essentially non-verbal and is, therefore, of necessity falsified by being put into words. But as a rationalist and a scientist, he really had no option but to try, since utilization of the already available techniques for handling unverbalizable, ineffable experiences, such as the *Via Negativa* of the mystics and the apophatic mode of argument of the theologians, would have seemed to him to be a betrayal of his life-long ideal, the creation of a truly scientific psychology, and of one of the basic assumptions of his generation, the assumption that the only real truths are scientific truths.

As this last paragraph will be obscure to all those readers who are even less versed in theology than I am, I must, I think, make its point a second time and in another way. Freud asserted that one of the major characteristics of the primary processes is that they are unconscious and in his early formulations he located them in a fictive space or area, which he designated negatively The Unconscious. And even when he changed this area's name to the Id, his description of it consisted largely of assertions of what it is not. 'It is the dark inaccessible part of our personality; what little we know of it we have learnt from our study of the dream-work and of the construction of neurotic symptoms, and most of that is of a negative character and can be described only as a contrast to the ego. We approach the id with analogies; we call it chaos, a cauldron. It is filled with energy reaching it from the instincts, but it has no organization, produces no collective will . . . the logical laws of thought do not apply . . . contrary impulses exist side by side without cancelling each other out. . . . There is nothing in the id that corresponds to the idea of time. . . . The id, of course, knows no judgements of value; no good and evil, no morality.'[1] Freud's Id has, in fact, one positive attribute, that of being filled with energy, but is otherwise defined negatively: it is unconscious, inaccessible, unorganized and has no sense of collective will, or logic, or contradiction, or time, or value, or good and evil, or morality.

So far as I know, the only other example of anyone proclaiming the existence of something profoundly important by asserting that it can only be approached with analogies and that it is not anything that can be defined positively is to be found in negative or apophatic theology, which asserts that human language, when applied to God, is inevitably inexact and inadequate and that it is therefore less misleading to use negative language about God than positive—'to refuse to say what God is, and to state simply what He is not.'[2] Curiously enough, the one positive attribute which negative theologians assert can be known about God is His energy, which again corresponds to Freud's account of the Id. However, my reason for mentioning negative theology here is not to discuss the parallels that can be drawn between the religious concept of God and the psychoanalytical concept of the Id, but to prepare the ground for arguing later that there is something about the imagination, in whatever guise it manifests itself, that can only be stated in negative terms.

Secondly, Freud formulated his theory of the primary and secondary processes in a cultural milieu very different from our own. He was born in 1856, he was in his early forties when he wrote *The Interpretation of Dreams*, and his formative years were, therefore, pre-Einstein, pre-Picasso, pre-Ezra Pound, pre-James Joyce. As a result it was natural for him to assume a much closer relationship between the verbal, the rational and the realistic on the one hand, and the non-verbal, the irrational and the imagined on the other hand, than anyone can today. He formulated his ideas before the visual arts had ceased to be representational and before literature had begun to explore the possibilities of fragmenting and manipulating the syntactical structure of language. He was therefore able to assume that when painters painted pictures, they were depicting objects and scenes that could, in principle, also be described in words, and that when writers wrote books, they were using language in essentially the same way as scientists do when they write learned treatises. As a result there appeared to him to be—and indeed given the historical context there was—nothing incongruous in assuming that of the two types of mental functioning he was describing, one, the verbal mode, was characteristic of the ego, of consciousness, of health, of rational adaptation to the environment, and the other, the non-verbal, iconic mode, was irrational and characteristic of dreamers, neurotics, lunatics, infants and primitive peoples; and that the capacity to use the former was dependent on repression of the latter.

In the event this idea that the primary processes are unconscious, primitive, neurotic, archaic and in normal people subject to repression, was to cause psychoanalysis considerable trouble, both in its theorizing and its public relations, since it soon became evident that there was some similarity between the imaginative activity displayed by artists and writers and the primary processes described by Freud as characteristic of dreaming and neurotic-symptom-formation. Given the clinical origins and bias of psychoanalysis, the easiest and most tempting way of explaining this similarity was to maintain that artists and writers are neurotic and that works of art are analogous to dreams and neurotic symptoms; and that the techniques of psychoanalytical interpretation can be transferred without modification to artists and their works.

This idea is still around today, despite Freud's rather belated disavowal of it in 1928.* It owes its vitality, I suspect, to four disparate sources. First, to envy—we are all envious of creative people and it is comforting to entertain the idea that they are not after all so very different from ourselves and that their gifts may not truly be gifts but bye-products of their neuroses. Secondly, to the pecking order that exists among academics and the intelligentsia generally: if scientists, and psychoanalysts almost universally claim to be scientists, could explain the creative imagination and slot it neatly into the scientific

---

* According to Jones, Freud made an even more extreme disavowal as early as 1912, when he wrote: 'Whence the artist derives his creative capacities is not a question for psychology.' However, the article in which it appeared was only published in Austria in 1924 and the first English translation only appeared in 1955. (The piece that caused all the trouble, Freud's 'Creative Writers and Day Dreaming', was published in 1908.)[3]

scheme of things, they would, at least in their own view, have one-upped the artists and enhanced their own prestige. Thirdly, to the rise of English Literature as an academic study and the concomitant expansion of the Ph.D industry, which has led to a demand in academic circles for new techniques to apply to the victims of literary thesis writers; and what more tempting than to add to literature's own critical armoury a few, mostly character-assassinating weapons borrowed from psychoanalysis. And fourthly, to the fact that there is indeed some similarity and connection between the creative imagination and dreaming, something long recognized by artists and writers themselves, and that it is, therefore, legitimate to discuss what the nature of this connection is.

Discussion of the relationship between waking imaginative activities and dreaming is, however, queered from the outset if one assumes, as many psychoanalysts still do, that in healthy, normal people the primary processes are repressed and that people in whom they are not repressed are ipso facto neurotic. The whole idea that artists and writers are neurotic and that dreaming is a universally occurring neurotic symptom stems, I suggest, from one simple but fallacious assumption, viz. that the primary processes and secondary processes are mutually antagonistic and that the former have, in health, to be relegated by repression to a curious underworld, The Repressed, The Unconscious or the Id. If this were true, then painters who can imagine what they intend to paint with quasi-hallucinatory, eidetic vividness and writers who can conjure up characters who seem to take on an independent life of their own would indeed be neurotic or psychotic.

But if one starts from another assumption, viz. that the primary and secondary processes co-exist from the beginning of life and that, in so far as repression and alienation do not intervene, they continue to function in harmony with one another, one providing the imaginative, the other the rational basis of living, creative people may be conceived to be those who retain into adult life something of that imaginative freedom which healthy, undiscouraged children display openly, but all too many lose as the shades of the prison-house begin to close upon them. 'A sharp and final division between the content of the two systems does not, as a rule, take place till puberty'[4] (Freud, 1915).

Thirdly, Freud's conception of the existence of unconscious primary processes was, in Freud's own view of the nature of science, profoundly unscientific. This seems only to have struck him forcibly when he came to consider the actual details of the imagery used by the primary processes and came to recognize the importance of symbolism in general and of sexual symbolism in particular. The first edition of his *The Interpretation of Dreams* (1900) had no section on symbolism in it and cites only one dream exemplifying sexual symbolism, and it was only in the fourth 1914 edition that a section on symbolism appeared for the first time. And even in the present *Standard Edition* the section on symbolism accounts for only 54 of its 623 pages.[5]

However, when Freud did eventually come to recognize the importance of symbolism, largely under the influence of Stekel, he was evidently embarrassed by the resistance of what he had encountered to the scientific method as he conceived it. Stekel, he wrote 'arrived at his interpretations of symbols by way of intuition, thanks to a peculiar gift for the direct understanding of them. But the existence of such a gift cannot be counted upon generally, its effectiveness is exempt from all criticism and consequently its findings have no claim to credibility . . . '[6] Although this is a very respectable scientific opinion, since questions of fact cannot indeed be arrived at by intuition but only by observation, the idea that intuition lacks all claim to credibility when applied to symbolism is fallacious and involves a category error, since symbols are not phenomena that can be observed and explained causally but metaphors used by people when they wish, for whatever reason, to allude to one thing by referring to another. Symbolism belongs in fact to the realm of the humanities, since it hinges on the fact that people can perceive similarities between things that are scientifically and rationally speaking dissimilar. And as Aristotle said 'a good metaphor implies an intuitive perception of the similarity in dissimilars'.[7]

As a result of his rejection of intuition on rational and scientific grounds, Freud had to cull evidence in support of symbolic interpretations of dream imagery from sources remote from the natural sciences on which he had hoped to build psychoanalysis. He had to turn to myths, to folk-lore, to anthropology, to etymology, to jokes, both clean and dirty, all 'soft' subjects from a natural scientific point of view. But what he discovered on these excursions into unfamiliar territory were not, I think, scientific facts about symbolism regarded as a mental phenomenon but evidence of a consensus in the way human beings imagine similarities between themselves and the not-self world, both animate and inanimate, around them.

If Freud had lived today, he would not, I think, have had to be embarrassed by the apparently non-scientific nature of this aspect of his discoveries, since the emergence of linguistics as a respectable scientific discipline would have enabled him to use that science as a model instead of neuro-anatomy. Instead of constructing a mental anatomy in which the primary processes were located in one part of a Psychic Apparatus and the secondary processes were located in another, he could have formulated a para-linguistic science, which might perhaps have been called oneirics, with iconic, structural and semantic branches, and containing sets of rules governing both the translation of oneiric, iconic utterances into verbal, phonetic statements and the setting up of obstacles and blocks against translation. In other words, the rules would have to be able to explain how, and under what conditions, dreams and neurotic symptoms can be understood and interpreted, and why, and under what conditions, they on occasion cannot be. Another set of rules would have to account for the fact that imagery related to biological destiny, which includes birth and death as well as sex, seems to occupy a central place in the lexigraphy of dreams.*

Although Freud unwittingly caused confusion about the role and status of the imagination in human existence by maintaining that dreams are like symptoms, that waking imaginative activities resemble dreams and neurotic phantasies, and that therefore creative people are like neurotics, poets and writers themselves seem always to have been clear that the imagination is the 'prime Agent', to use Coleridge's phrase, of their creative activity and that some important connection and resemblance exists between dreaming and their waking creative activities. It would be possible to cite innumerable examples of writers who have used their dreams as the initial source of their inspiration, who have claimed, sometimes untruthfully, to have composed poems in their sleep, who have recorded their dreams in their working notebooks, who have included dreams they have had in the text of their novels, who have claimed to be specifically 'dreamers of dreams'. These facts are, however, too well known to bear repetition here, so instead I shall re-quote what Charles Darwin had to say about dreams and the imagination.

> The Imagination is one of the highest prerogatives of man. By this faculty he unites former images and ideas, independently of the will, and thus creates brilliant and novel results. A poet, as Jean Paul Richter remarks, 'who must reflect whether he shall make a character say yes or no—to the devil with him; he is only a stupid corpse.' Dreaming gives us the best notion of this power; as Jean Paul again says, 'The dream is an involuntary kind of poetry.'[8]

This passage comes from Darwin's *The Descent of Man*, which was first published in 1871, over twenty years before Freud wrote his *The Interpretation of Dreams*. It is striking that both

* Lexigraphy—a system of writing in which each character represents a word (*Shorter Oxford English Dictionary*.)

Darwin and Richter emphasize the imagination's independence of the will, a matter to which I shall return later.

The first and the most obvious similarity between dreams and products of the literary imagination is that they can be granted or refused meaning according to the predilection of the person who has, hears or reads them. This is obviously so in the case of dreams. Despite Freud, it is probably true that the majority of educated people in Britain, though perhaps not in the United States, do not attribute any meaning to dreams and regard them as nonsensical or as analogous to the 'noise' made by electronic equipment when it is switched on but not actually working. It is, however, less obvious that it is possible to deny meaning to poems and novels. And yet we all know people who, despite being literate, are literal-minded and unimaginative, who don't really get the point of novels and poems and are flummoxed by the fact that the realm or order of reality to which they should be assigned is not readily defined or located; who are flummoxed by precisely that imaginative element in fiction which makes it impossible to categorize novels as simply disguised autobiography or disguised sociology, and who don't really understand why poems need to be laid out on the page in such a wasteful, extravagant manner.

If, however, one does assign meaning to dreams, novels and poems, they immediately acquire not one single meaning, but multiple and manifold meanings. Unlike factual statements like 'The Battle of Waterloo took place on June 18th, 1815' or 'Arsenic is a poison' which have only one meaning, dreams poems and novels either have no meaning or several meanings. Once one has recognized, detected or decided that they have meaning, they become open to interpretation, and characteristically several not mutually exclusive interpretations can be made of them. Characteristically, too, exegesis of these interpretations takes up more space, and uses more words, than does the dream, poem or even the novel itself. This is due, of course, to the fact that the imagination unites, to use Darwin's word, or condenses, to use Freud's word, numbers of images and themes into a unitary whole, which therefore takes up less space than the individual items do if enumerated in series.

In a volume of essays entitled *Interpretations*[9] edited by John Wain, it takes Dennis Ward thirteen pages to answer the question 'What did the sonnet "The Windhover" mean to Gerard Manley Hopkins?', i.e. just under a page to a line. Furthermore, his answer involves him in mentioning at least ten verbally distinguishable meanings for one of the poem's two central images, the falcon—the other central image is the air or wind which sustains it in flight—even though these ten meanings fuse in the poem itself to form one meaning which it is artificial to dissect out into sub-meanings.

A further similarity between dreams and products of the waking imagination is, as Darwin mentions in the passage I quoted earlier, that their production is independent of the will. We do not make up or construct our dreams; they occur or happen to us, and while we are dreaming we do not recognize that we are ourselves the agent creating the dream. The same seems to be true of at least the initial idea or impetus of any literary work; it just comes to the writer or poet. A necessary precondition of all imaginative activity seems to be what Keats called 'negative capability', the ability to allow oneself to be 'in uncertainties, mysteries, doubts, without any irritable reaching after fact and reason'; a state of mind the exact opposite to that of the healthy, well-adapted ego sanctified by Freudian theory. And, at least for some writers, the execution as well as the conception of their work may also be largely independent of the will. Coleridge claimed that Kubla Khan came to him in his sleep, though his decision to write it down after awakening must have been an act of will, and Enid Blyton has left a vivid account of how her characters took over while she was writing her books.

I shut my eyes for a few minutes, with my portable type-writer on my knee—I make my mind blank and wait—and then, as clearly as I would see real children, my characters stand before me in my mind's eye. I see them in detail—hair, eyes, feet, clothes, expression—and I always know their Christian names but never their surnames. . . . I don't know what anyone is going to say or do. I don't know what is going to happen. I am in the happy position of being able to write a story and read it for the first time, at one and the same moment. . . . Sometimes a character makes a joke, a really funny one, that makes me laugh as I type it on my paper—and I think, 'Well, I couldn't have thought of that myself in a hundred years!' And then I think, 'Well, who *did* think of it, then?'[10]

Although I have no particular wish to sing Enid Blyton's praises, it must be admitted that her question 'Well, who *did* think of it, then?' is an extremely good one, and that she was far from being what Jean Paul Richter called a stupid corpse who had to reflect whether she should make a character say yes or no. This fact that in creative writing the self who writes is not the same self as the 'I' of one's routine being and that it creates independently of the will, a fact which Enid Blyton seems to have discovered with startling and refreshing naïveté, is presumably why poets and writers before the rise of rationalism could believe that their imagination was literally inspired by a God or a Muse—and why when science turned its attention to dreaming, it had to postulate an impersonal agent, an Id, or It, or Unconscious, at work behind the scenes. It is also the reason why we withhold full artistic authenticity to works of art that strike us as contrived, fanciful or *voulu*.

But despite these similarities between the ways in which the imagination manifests itself in dreams and in works of literary art, there are, of course, numerous differences, some of which arise from the fact that people are asleep when they dream and awake when they write, and others from the fact that dreams are private self-to-self communications while at some point in the creation of a poem or novel the author's conception of its likely or hoped-for readers will enter into its composition.

Quite apart from the fact that dreams, as actually experienced during sleep, are more like moving pictures than passages of print, they are, as a result, in general less organized, less, unified, indeed less condensed than works of art; they more often resemble someone who is groping for the appropriate metaphor than someone who has found it. Even if one accepts Richter's dictum, quoted earlier, that dreams are an involuntary kind of poetry, one has to add that they are usually also an uncompleted kind of poetry. Something would still need to be done to them before they could be transferred from the private sector of experience to the public, before they could acquire universality.

This something-still-to-be-done cannot, I think, be the tidying-up and ordering of the dream until it fulfils the formal requirements of a work of art, but must rather comprise the casting of the central meaning in symbols which are part of the shared iconography of the culture of which the poet or writer is a member, and which, therefore, carry a heavy charge of shared public associations and resonances. And although people may on occasion dream dreams which satisfy this requirement and which could, therefore, be converted into a poem—or a painting—in general the imagery used by the dream imagination is too private, too idiosyncratic, too ephemeral, and too dependent on the dreamer's intimate biography for dreams to be convertible into works of art of universal or even wide appeal

Gerard Manley Hopkins' 'The Windhover',[11] for instance, fuses images derived not from his private experience but from ornithology, falconry, skating, chivalry, and Christianity—all public images with which any literate person could well be familiar—to make a personal statement about the relationship between divine inspiration, symbolized by the Wind, and human aspiration, symbolized by the hovering Falcon. Interestingly enough, if it were permissible to equate Hopkin's God with Freud's Id, it would be possible to interpret 'The Windhover' as a statement about the dynamic interdependence of the Ego and the Id, although I have a feeling that Hopkins would have had greater sympathy with Jung's and Groddeck's conception of the relationship between I and It than Freud's.

But I have stated my last point positively when I should have stated it negatively. It is not that the poet and writer actively masters the imagery and iconography of his times in order to be able to universalize his private emotions, in order to convert his dreams into works of art, but that one aspect of his 'negative capability' is an exceptional sensitivity and receptivity to the symbolic, iconic network that constitutes the culture he inhabits, which makes it natural for him to express his private emotions in universal terms—or, indeed, perhaps not to distinguish between the universal and the individual, between the macrocosm of human destiny and the microcosm of his individual ego.

It is, indeed, my impression that people who possess negative capability to a high degree seem not to conceive of themselves as an Ego opposed to an alien environment and an alien Unconscious both of which they have to master by 'irritably reaching after fact and reason', but rather as a part of the universe which is capable of absorbing the whole into itself and then recreating it by distillation in imaginative works; in other and psycho-analytical words, their relationship to 'external reality' is identificatory without impermeable 'ego-boundaries' drawn between themselves and others or between their 'I' and their 'It'. They also seem to be refreshingly free from the conventional notion that activity is masculine and passivity is feminine and can therefore oscillate between active and passive states of being, and between objectivity and subjectivity, without feeling that their identity is threatened by doing so.

To conclude, dreaming and waking imaginative activity resemble one another in that they both create 'novel results' (Darwin's phrase) by uniting, condensing and fusing images and ideas already present in the mind, in that they do so independently of the will, and in that their meaning, when they can be seen to have one, is always multiple and manifold. Furthermore, the self or agent that creates them is not the 'I' or Ego that opposes itself to the rest of the universe but some wider, less personal self to which the 'I' has to abandon itself, in the case of dreaming by falling asleep, in the case of waking imaginative activity by attainment of that receptive state of mind which Keats called Negative Capability. Although dreaming is an imaginative activity and dreams can be interpreted, dreaming only rarely produces novel results of universal appeal or significance, since the imagery used in dreams is usually too private and too dependent on the dreamer's intimate biography to be publicly comprehensible. Creative people who possess the capacity for negative capability in high degree seem to conceive of themselves as part of the macrocosm and to lack that sense of opposition between their Ego and both the outside world and their own unconscious which renders the majority resistive to their own imaginative potentialities. This enables them to allow themselves to make imaginative statements which have both private and universal meaning. Freud's theory of the primary and secondary processes explains correctly what happens to imagery during imaginative activity but Freud's assumption that the primary processes are neurotic, primitive and unrealistic and are repressed in healthy people insinuates the idea that both dreaming and creative waking activities are in principle neurotic. This is why in earlier sections of this book I have preferred to use Susanne Langer's distinction between discursive and non-discursive symbolism.

Finally, this last chapter, and indeed many earlier sections of this book, constitutes an attempt to marry Coleridge's Theory of the Poetic Imagination and Freud's theory of dreams —without, I hope, doing too much violence to either.

Postscript

It occurred to me, at a late stage in the writing of this book, that I had made nine specific points about the psychology of dreams; that four of them were patently disagreements with Freud's theory of dreams, three were irreconcilable with Jung's view of them, and five were elaborations or reformulations of Freudian ideas, or were nor-nor-West of both Freud and Jung. But I would like to make it plain that I have no wish to lumber the world with yet another theory of dreams. My aim has rather been to record some of the reflections, impressions and ideas that have been forced upon me by three decades of listening to other people's dreams, of reading learned papers about the psychology of dreams and the physiology of dreaming—and, of course, by more than three decades of myself falling asleep, dreaming, and, on occasion, remembering what I have dreamt.

This experience of sustained diurnal exposure to the dreams of others and nocturnal exposure to my own has led me to believe that dreams are best understood, even in a clinical setting, if one forgets all theories about them and ceases to think of them as discrete phenomena or items of experience, but instead responds to them as glimpses of the dreamer's total imaginative fabric; that dreams cannot possibly be either discharges of instinctual tension or attempts to communicate with others but must be self-communings; and that dreaming must be an activity of which we are inevitably to an extent innnocent, partly because there is more to the imagination than any individual moment of consciousness can apprehend, and partly because it bears a relationship to conscious selfhood analogous to that of the Wind to the Windhover it sustains in flight—omnipresent and yet not in its particularities perceptible.

The Windhover is, indeed, the central image of this book. It has been at the back of my mind even when no glimpse of it has appeared on the page. Gerard Manley Hopkins must, therefore, have the last word.

> I caught this morning morning's minion, king-
> dom of daylight's dauphin, dapple-dawn-drawn Falcon,
>   in his riding
> Of the rolling level underneath him steady air, and
>   striding
> High there, how he rung upon the rein of a wimpling wing
> In his ecstasy! then off, off forth on swing,
> As a skate's heel sweeps smooth on a bow-bend: the hurl
>   and gliding
> Rebuffed the big wind. My heart in hiding
> Stirred for a bird,—the achieve of, the mastery of the
> thing!
>
> Brute beauty and valour and act, oh, air pride, plume, here
> Buckle! AND the fire that breaks from thee then, a
>   billion
> Times told lovelier, more dangerous. O my chevalier!
>
> No wonder of it: sheer plod makes plough down sillion
> Shine, and blue-bleak embers, ah my dear,
> Fall, gall themslves, and gash gold-vermillion.

Notes

Introduction

1. B. D. Lewin, *Dreams and the Uses of Regression* (International Universities Press, New York, 1958) p. 11.

2. In 'Causes and Meaning', the Introduction to *Psychoanalysis Observed* (Constable, London, 1966; Coward–McCann, New York, 1967). Cf. also H. J. Home's 'The Concept of Mind', *Int. J. Psycho-Anal.*, 1966, Vol. 47, pp. 42–9, and Thomas Szasz's *The Myth of Mental Illness* (Secker & Warburg, London, 1962; Harper & Row, New York, 1961).

3. See Gregory Bateson, *Steps to an Ecology of Mind* (Paladin, London, 1973; Chandler–Davis, New Jersey, 1972), Part IV, 'Epistemology and Ecology'.

Chapter 1
Freud's Theory of Dreams

1. S. Freud, *The Interpretation of Dreams*, in *The Standard Edition of the Complete Psychological Works of Sigmund Freud*,* Vol. IV, p. 678.

2. S. Freud, *On Dreams*, in *Standard Edition*, Vol. V, p. 678.

3. S. Freud, *The Interpretation of Dreams*, op. cit.

4. *Ibid.*, p. 582. 'Since I have asserted that neurotic anxiety arises from sexual sources . . .' and 'Anxiety in dreams, I should like to insist, is an anxiety problem and not a dream problem.'

5. *Ibid.*, Ch. VII; 'Formulations on the Two Principles of Mental Functioning', *Standard Edition*, Vol. XII; 'Papers on Metapsychology', *Standard Edition*, Vol. XIV. Strictly speaking, symbolization is not one of the primary processes, since it can be broken down into displacement and condensation, but most analysts other than Freud himself have treated it as one.

6. S. Freud, *New Introductory Lectures on Psycho-Analysis*, in *Standard Edition*, Vol. XXII.

* Published by The Hogarth Press, London, 1953–74; W. W. Norton, New York. Henceforward abbreviated as *Standard Edition*.

7. See my paper 'Beyond the Reality Principle' in *Imagination and Reality* (Hogarth Press, London, 1968; International Universities Press, New York) for a detailed criticism of Freud's view of the relationship between the primary and secondary processes and for references to the relevant literature.

8. S. Freud, 'Dostoevsky and Parricide', *Standard Edition*, Vol. XXI.

9. For the irrelevance of the concept of energy to psychoanalysis see John Bowlby, *Attachment and Loss*, Vol. 1, 'Attachment' (Hogarth Press, London, 1969; Basic Books, New York), pp. 13–23. For the suggestion that Freud's theory of mental energy was really a theory of meaning in disguise, see the entry 'Energy' in my *A Critical Dictionary of Psychoanalysis* (Nelson, London, 1968; Basic Books, New York, 1969).

10. Susanne K. Langer, *Philosophy in a New Key* (Harvard, Cambridge, Mass., 1951), pp. 96–7.

11. Ella F. Sharpe, *Dream Analysis* (Hogarth Press, London, 1937; new edition 1978; Brunner Mazel, New York, 1978).

12. *Aristotle on the Art of Poetry*. A revised text with critical introduction, translation and commentary by Ingram Bywater (Oxford University Press, London, 1909; New York, 1920), Ch. 22.

13. *The Ego and the Id*, in *Standard Edition*, Vol. XIX.

14. From a letter from Groddeck to Freud, 27.5.1917, quoted in Georg Groddeck, *The Meaning of Illness* (Hogarth Press, London, 1977; Int. Univ. Press, New York), p. 33.

15. S. Freud, *An Outline of Psycho-Analysis*, in *Standard Edition*, Vol. XXIII.

16. Ernest Jones, 'Freud's Theory of Dreams' (1910), in *Papers on Psycho-Analysis* (Baillière, London, 1948).

17. 'Remarks on the Theory and Practice of Dream-Interpretation', in *Standard Edition*, Vol. XIX.

18. 'Freud's Theory of Dreams', in *Papers on Psycho-Analysis* (Baillière, London, 1948).

19. *The Interpretation of Dreams, op. cit.*, p. 542.

20. *Ibid.*, p. 542. The quotation from Hobbes is from the *Leviathan*.

21. *Ibid.*, p. 543.

22. *Ibid.*, p. 548.

23. *Ibid.*, p. 548.

24. *Ibid.*, p. 543.

25. *Ibid.*, p. 546.

26. Francis Galton, *Inquiries into Human Faculty and its Development* (Macmillan, London, 1883; reprinted by AMS Press, New York).

27. S. Freud, *Introductory Lectures on Psycho-Analysis*, in *Standard Edition*, Vol. XVI, pp. 456–7.

28. *The Interpretation of Dreams, op. cit.*, p. 107.

29. *Ibid.*, pp. 106–21.

30. *Ibid.*, pp. 118–19.

31. P. J. Mahoney, 'Towards a Formalist Approach to Dreams', *Int. Rev. Psycho-Anal.* (1977), Vol. IV, Pt. 1.

Chapter 2
Jung's View of Dreams

1. Quoted by Jolande Jacobi in *The Psychology of C. G. Jung* (Routledge, London, 1951; Yale University Press, New Haven, 1951), from *Die Wirklichkeit der Seele*, p. 88.

2. Quoted by Jolande Jacobi from *Seminar on Children's Dreams, 1938–9.*

3. *Ibid.*

4. C. G. Jung, *Modern Man in Search of a Soul* (Routledge, London, 1933; Harcourt, New York, 1933).

5. Calvin S. Hall, *The Meaning of Dreams* (McGraw-Hill, New York, 1966).

6. C. G. Jung, *Memories, Dreams, Reflections* (Fontana, London, 1963; Pantheon Books, New York, 1963).

7. E. A. Bennet, *What Jung Really Said* (Macdonald, London, 1966; Schocken Books, New York, 1967), p. 88–9.

8. Plato, *The Republic*, Bk ix. Quoted by H. G. McCurdy, 'The History of Dream Theory', 1946, *Psychol. Rev.*, Vol. 53.

9. Quoted by E. A. Bennet from *The Practice of Psychotherapy, The Collected Works of C. G. Jung*, Vol. XVI (Routledge, London; Princeton University Press, Bollingen Series, Vol. 16, Princeton, New Jersey, 1966).

10. E. A. Bennet, *op. cit.*, pp. 86–7.

11. C. G. Jung, *Man and His Symbols* (Aldus, London, 1964; Doubleday, New York, 1964).

12. Quoted by E. A. Bennet from *The Structure and Dynamics of the Psyche, The Collected Works of C. G. Jung*, Vol. VIII (Routledge, London; Princeton University Press, New Jersey).

13. Quoted by E. A. Bennet from 'C. G. Jung: Fundamental Psychological Conceptions'. Seminar given in London, 1938.

NOTES

Chapter 3
Imagination, Dreaming and the Self

1. See I. A. Richards, *Coleridge on Imagination* (Routledge, London, 1950; W. W. Norton, New York, 1950). The crucial quotation from the *Biographia Literaria* (1817) defining primary and secondary imagination is given on pp. 57–8.

2. See Ch. 1, section 11.

3. Charles Darwin, *The Descent of Man* (Murray, London, 1871), p. 74.

4. I. A. Richards, *op. cit.*, p. 58.

5. For confirmation of these statements see Ch. 5 section 6, and Ch. 5 section 10.

6. *John Keats, Letters*, ed. M. B. Forman (Oxford University Press, London and New York, 1935). This extract comes from Letter 32, to G. and T. Keats.

7. Theodor Reik, *Surprise and the Psycho-Analyst* (Hogarth Press, London, 1936).

8. Kilton Stewart, 'Dream Theory in Malaya' in Charles T. Start (ed.) *Altered States of Consciousness* (Wiley, New York, 1969). 'The interpretation of dreams is a feature of child education and is part of the shared knowledge of the Senoi tribe. It is practised by the ordinary Senoi as a feature of his daily life. The breakfast in the Senoi house is like a dream clinic, in the words of Kilton Stewart, with the elder males hearing and analyzing the dreams of their children.' Robert E. Ornstein, *The Psychology of Consciousness* (Penguin, Harmondsworth, 1975).

9. Calvin S. Hall, *The Meaning of Dreams* (McGraw–Hill, New York, 1966), p. 12.

10. Lorenz, M., and Cobb, S., Language Behaviour in Psychoneurotic Patients', *Arch. Neurol. Psychiat.*, 1953, Vol. 69; Lorenz, M., 'Language as Expressive Behaviour', *Arch. Neurol. Psychiat.*, Vol. 70.

11. Calvin S. Hall, *op. cit.* This book claims to be based on the study of thousands of dreams collected from hundreds of normal people.

12. Roy Schafer, *A New Language for Psychoanalysis* (Yale, New Haven and London, 1976).

13. *The Meaning of Dreams*, p. 11.

14. *The Interpretation of Dreams*, in *Standard Edition*, Vol. V, p. 351.

15. Wilhelm Reich, *Character Analysis* (Vision Press, London, 1969). See also my *Reich* (Fontana, London, 1971).

16. D. W. Winnicott, *Through Paediatrics to Psycho-Analysis* (Hogarth Press, London, 1975; New York, Basic Books), pp. 71–2, 281.

17. C. G. Jung, *The Structure and Dynamics of the Psyche, Collected Works* (Routledge, London; Princeton University Press, New Jersey), Vol. VIII, p. 292. 'But since everything living strives for wholeness, the inevitable onesidedness of our conscious life is continually being corrected and compensated by the universal human being in us, whose goal is the ultimate integration of conscious and unconscious, or better, the assimilation of the ego to a wider personality.'

18. Quoted by Kathleen Coburn, *The Self-Conscious Imagination* (Oxford University Press, 1974). The notebook reference is CN III 4066.

Chapter 4
Metaphor and Symbol

1. Aristotle, *The Art of Poetry*, translated by Ingram Bywater (Oxford University Press, 1909), Ch. 22.

2. H. W. Fowler, *A Dictionary of Modern English Usage* (Oxford University Press), p. 359.

3. Thomas Nash(e), *Summer's Last Will and Testament*. See William Empson, *Seven Types of Ambiguity* (Penguin, Harmondsworth, 1961), p. 25.

4. Ernest Jones, 'The Theory of Symbolism', in *Papers on Psycho-Analysis* (Baillière, London, 1948).

5. L. S. Kubie, 'The Distortion of the Symbolic Process in Neurosis and Psychosis', *J. Amer. Psychoanal. Assoc.*, Vol. 1, 1953. Other analysts who have questioned Jones's theory of symbolism are Marion Milner in 'Aspects of Symbolism in Comprehension of the Not-Self', *Int. J. Psycho-Anal.*, Vol. XXXIII, 1952; Hanna Segal in 'Notes on Symbol Formation', *Int. J. Psycho-Anal.*, Vol. XXXVIII, 1957; and myself in Ch. 4. of *Imagination and Reality* (Hogarth Press, London, 1968; International Universities Press, New York).

6. S. Freud, *Introductory Lectures on Psycho-Analysis*, in *Standard Edition*, Vol. XVI.

7. See also my article 'Is Freudian Symbolism a Myth?' in *Symbols and Sentiments*, edited by Ioan Lewis (Academic Press, London, 1977).

8. Marion Milner, 'Aspects of Symbolism in Comprehension of the Not-Self' in *Int. J. Psycho-Anal.*, Vol. XXXIII, 1952.

NOTES

9. This dream is analysed in greater detail in Ch. 2 of my *Imagination and Reality* (*op cit.*)

10. S. Freud, *Introductory Lectures*, in *Standard Edition*, Vol. XV, p. 153.

11. Otto Rank, *The Trauma of Birth* (Kegan Paul, London, 1929).

12. Calvin S. Hall, *The Meaning of Dreams* (McGraw–Hill, New York, 1966).

13. S. Freud, *Introductory Lectures*, in *Standard Edition*, Vol. XV, p. 158.

15. C. G. Jung, *Memories, Dreams, Reflections* (Fontana, London, 1963; Pantheon Books, New York).

16. See the dream and symbol indexes in Vols. V, XVI and XXIV of *Standard Edition*.

17. *Introductory Lectures on Psycho-Analysis*, in *Standard Edition*, Vol. XV, pp. 156–8.

Chapter 5
Various Types of Dreams

1. See also Ch. 2 of my *Anxiety and Neurosis* (Allen Lane, London, 1968); and Martha Wolfenstein, *Disaster* (Glencoe, 1957).

2. Ernest L. Hartmann, 'A Note on the Nightmare', in *Sleep and Dreaming, International Psychiatry Clinics*, Vol. VII (New York, 1970).

3. David Foulkes et. al., 'Two Studies of Childhood Dreaming', *Amer. J. Orthopsychiat.*, Vol. XXXIX, 1969.

4. Ernest Jones, *On the Nightmare* (Hogarth Press, London, 1949; Liveright, New York).

5. *Ibid.*, p. 39.

6. Ernest Jones, 'The Unconscious Mind and Medical Practice' in *Papers on Psycho-Analysis* (Baillière, London, 1948), p. 356.

7. Charles Rycroft, *Anxiety and Neurosis* (Allen Lane, London, 1968).

8. H. S. Liddell, *Emotional Hazards in Animals and Man* (Thomas, Springfield, Illinois, 1956).

9. William McDougall, *An Introduction to Social Psychology* (Methuen, London, 1931).

10. *Introductory Lectures on Psycho-Analysis*, in *Standard Edition*, Vol. XVI, Lecture XIV.

11. *The Interpretation of Dreams*, in *Standard Edition*, Vol. V, p. 580.

12. *Ibid.*, p. 582.

13. 'Analysis of a Phobia in a Five Year-Old Boy' in *Standard Edition*, Vol. X, pp. 23–6.

175

14. In *The Ego and the Id*, in *Standard Edition*, Vol. XIX.

15. Calvin S. Hall, *The Meaning of Dreams* (McGraw–Hill, New York, 1966).

16. Ian Oswald, *Sleep* (Penguin, Harmondsworth, 1966).

17. Calvin S. Hall, *op. cit.*, p. 49.

18. O'Reilly has here misquoted Horace. *The Oxford Dictionary of Quotations* gives *Naturam expellas furca, tamen usque recurret* (if you drive nature with a pitchfork, she will soon find a way back). I doubt whether any contemporary surgeon, which is what Sir Astley Cooper (d. 1841) was, would be prepared to express himself so definitely on such a matter as Sir Astley seems to have done.

19. Ernest Jones, *On the Nightmare, op. cit.*, p. 88.

20. Calvin S. Hall, *op. cit.* The quotation comes from the introduction where he is discussing research about to be done at the Institute of Dream Research, Santa Cruz, California.

21. P. Neubauer, 'Children's Dreams', Ch. 20 of *The Child: His Psychological and Cultural Development*, Vol. I, ed. A. M. Freedman and H. I. Kaplan (New York, 1972).

22. Ernest Jones, 'Freud's Theory of Dreams' in *Papers on Psycho-Analysis* (Baillière, London, 1958).

23. David Foulkes *et al.*, *op. cit.*

24. Ann Faraday, *Dream Power* (Pan, London, 1972).

25. Gregory Bateson *et al.* 'Towards a Theory of Schizophrenia', *Behavioural Science*, Vol. I, 1956; reprinted in *Steps to an Ecology of Mind* (Paladin, London, 1973).

26. R. D. Laing, *Sanity, Madness and the Family* (Tavistock, London, 1970); *The Politics of the Family* (Tavistock, London, 1971).

27. John Bowlby, *Attachment and Loss*, Vol. II, 'Separation' (Hogarth Press, London, 1973; Basic Books, New York), Ch. 20.

28. Ch. 3. of *Imagination and Reality* (Hogarth Press, London, 1968; International Universities Press, New York).

29. B. D. Lewin, 'Sleep, the Mouth and the Dream Screen', *Psychoanal. Quart.*, Vol. XV, 1946.

30. Charles Rycroft, 'A Contribution to the Study of the Dream Screen', *Int. J. Psycho-Anal.*, Vol. XXXII, 1951, reprinted as Ch. I of *Imagination and Reality, op. cit.* J. B. Boyer, 'A Hypothesis regarding the Time of Appearance of the Dream Screen', *Int. J. Psycho-Anal*, Vol. XLI, 1960.

31. R. C. Zaehner, *Mysticism: Sacred and Profane* (Oxford, 1957).

32. Ian Oswald, *Sleep, op. cit.*

33. *The Interpretation of Dreams*, in *Standard Edition*, Vol. V, pp. 408–9.

34. Ella F. Sharpe, *Dream Analysis* (Hogarth Press, London, 1937; new edition 1978: Brunner Mazel, New York).

35. *Ibid.*

Chapter 6
Sleep and the Physiology of Dreams

1. Aserinsky, E., and Kleitman, N., 'Regularly Occurring Periods of Eye Motility and Concomitant Phenomena during Sleep', *Science*, Vol. CXVIII, 1953.

2. B. D. Lewin, 'Sleep, the Mouth and the Dream Screen' *Psychoanal. Quart.*, Vol. XV, 1946. *The Psychoanalysis of Elation* (Hogarth Press, London, 1951; W. W. Norton, New York, 1950).

3. Ernest L. Hartmann, *The Functions of Sleep* (Yale, Newhaven, 1973).

4. J. H. Jackson, 'Evolution and Dissolution of the Nervous System' (1884) in *Selected Writings* (Staples, London, 1958; Basic Books, New York), pp. 45–75.

5. See Roger Shattock, *Marcel Proust* (Fontana, London, 1974; Viking Press, New York).

6. Wilkie Collins, *Basil* (Bentley, London, 1852).

7. Kenneth Robinson, *Wilkie Collins* (Bodley Head, London, 1951; Macmillan, New York), and see Ch. 9 of my *Imagination and Reality* (Hogarth Press, London, 1968; International Universities Press, New York).

8. M. D. Austin, 'Dream Recall and the Bias of Intellectual Ability', *Nature*, Vol. 231, 7.5.71. See also Liam Hudson, *Contrary Imaginations* (Methuen, London, 1966; Schocken Books, New York).

9. William C. Dement, 'The Biological Role of REM Sleep (circa 1968) in A. Kales (ed.), *Sleep: Physiology and Pathology* (Lippincott, New York, 1969).

10. See F. Snyder, 'Towards an Evolutionary Theory of Dreaming', *Am. J. Psychiat.*, Vol. CXXIII, 1966.

11. Calvin S. Hall, *The Meaning of Dreams* (McGraw–Hill, New York, 1966).

12. Ralph J. Berger, 'Experimental Modification of Dream Content by Meaningful Verbal Stimuli', *Brit. J. Psychiat.*, Vol. CIX, 1963.

13. Charles Fisher *et al.*, 'Cycle of Penile Erection Synchronous with Dreaming (REM) Sleep', *Archives of General Psychiatry*, Vol. XII, 1965.

Chapter 7
Dream Incubation and Visitations

1. J. S. Lincoln, *The Dream in Primitive Cultures* (Cresset, London, 1935; William Wood, Baltimore, 1936).
2. B. Malinowski, *Sex and Repression in Savage Society* (Harcourt Brace, New York, 1927).
3. These quotations from Macrobius have been taken from A. C. Spearing, *Medieval Dream-Poetry* (Cambridge University Press, London and Cambridge, Mass., 1976). Spearing's book is concerned not with the dreams that medieval man actually dreamt but with the use medieval poets made of prevailing ideas about dreams.
4 *The Oneirocritica of Artemidorus.* Translation and Commentary by Robert J. White (Noyes Press, New Jersey, 1975).
5. 'When the Sleeper Awakes'. Review in *Times Literary Supplement*, 23.4.76.
6. Ch. 10 of E. R. Dodds, *The Ancient Concept of Progress* (Oxford, 1973).
7. E. R. Dodds, *The Greeks and the Irrational* (Berkeley, 1951).
8. David Bakan, *Sigmund Freud and the Jewish Mystical Tradition* (Schocken Books, New York, 1965).

Chapter 9
Dreams and the Literary Imagination

1. S. Freud, *New Introductory Lectures on Psycho-Analysis*, in *Standard Edition*, Vol. XXII.
2. Timothy Ware, *The Orthodox Church* (Penguin, Harmondsworth, 1963; Peter Smith, Gloucester, Mass., 1964).
3. S. Freud, 'Creative Writers and Day Dreaming' in *Standard Edition*, Vol. IX.
4. S. Freud, 'Papers on Metapsychology', in *Standard Edition*, Vol. XIV.
5. S. Freud, *The Interpretation of Dreams*, in *Standard Edition*, Vol. V, pp. 350–404.
6. *Ibid.*, p. 350.
7. Aristotle, *The Art of Poetry*, translated by Ingram Bywater (Oxford, 1909), Ch. 22.
8. Charles Darwin, *The Descent of Man* (Murray, London, 1871).
9. John Wain (ed.), *Interpretations: Essays on Twelve English Poems* (Routledge, London, 1957; Hilary House, New York).

NOTES

10. Barbara Stoney, *Enid Blyton: a Biography* (Hodder, London, 1974).

11. From *Poems 1876–1889*, in *Selected Poems of Gerard Manley Hopkins* (Heinemann, London, 1953).

Postscript

1. From *Poems 1876–1889*, in *Selected Poems of Gerard Manley Hopkins* (Heinemann, London, 1953). Also in *The Poems of Gerard Manley Hopkins* edited by W. H. Gardner and N. H. MacKenzie (Oxford University Press, fourth edition 1967).

INDEX

INDEX

INDEX